AMERICAN CORPORATE IDENTITY 2004

Edited by
David E. Carter

AMERICAN CORPORATE IDENTITY 2004
Copyright © 2003 by David E. Carter and HDI, an imprint of
HarperCollins*Publishers*.

First published in 2003 by:
Harper Design International,
An imprint of HarperCollins*Publishers*
10 East 53rd Street
New York, NY 10022

Distributed throughout the world by:
HarperCollins International
10 East 53rd Street
New York, NY 10022
Fax: (212) 207-7654

HarperCollins books may be purchased for educational, business,
or sales promotional use. For information, please write: Special
Markets Department, HarperCollins Publishers Inc., 10 East 53rd
Street, New York, NY 10022.

Library of Congress Control Number: 2003104638

ISBN: 0-06-053613-6

Printed in Hong Kong by Everbest Printing Company through
Four Colour Imports, Louisville, Kentucky.
First Printing, 2003

TABLE OF CONTENTS

COMPLETE
CORPORATE IDENTITY
PROGRAMS

ExForum

ExForum

CLIENT
FedExForum
DESIGN FIRM
Landor Associates
DESIGNERS
Rafael Baeza, Graham Atkinson,
Rachel Wear, Margaret Youngblood,
Tom Venegas

ExForum

CLIENT
Belz Enterprise
DESIGN FIRM
ID8 Studio/RTKL
DESIGNERS
Phil Engelke, Thom McKay,
Jill Popowich, Frank Christian,
Cindy Reppert-Ault, Matt Weisgerber

THE STREETS AT SOUTHPOINT

CLIENT
Urban Retail Properties
DESIGN FIRM
ID8 Studio/RTKL
DESIGNERS
Damon Robinson, Erin Ryan, Lon Calvert,
Cheri Wysong, Josh Eiowsky, Damon Bakun,
Frank Christian, Jill Popowich

CLIENT
Mercy Medical Center
DESIGN FIRM
ID8 Studio/RTKL
DESIGNERS
Greg Rose, Phil Engelke

PRINCESS
where i belong®

CLIENT
  Princess Cruises
DESIGN FIRM
  Sargent & Berman
DESIGNERS
  Peter Sargent, Barbara Chan,
  Jelina Saurenman, Melissa Ballard

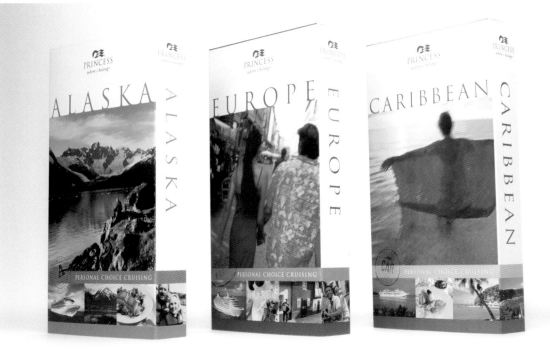

XIAMETER™ *The new measure of value. From Dow Corning.*

CLIENT
Xiameter
DESIGN FIRM
Landor Associates
DESIGNERS
Matteo Vianello, Michele Berry,
Dean Wilcox, Margaret Youngblood,
Steve Ensminger, Ping-Ki Chan,
Liz Magnusson, Kristin Lanham

Seagate

We turn on ideas

Mobile Technology

AT VERO EOS ET ACCUSAM ET IUSTO
ODOGIODIGNISSUM QUI BLANDIT PAESENT

CLIENT
Seagate Technologies, Inc.
DESIGN FIRM
Landor Associates
DESIGNERS
Anastasia Laksmi, Michele Berry,
Josh Hittleman, Sylvain Gilliand,
Ivan Thelin, Rebecca Titcomb,
Dean Wilcox, Nicolas Aparicio,
Susan Davis, Brian Green, Marco Ugolini,
Tin Chu, Russell DeHaven, Cynthia Elliott

CLIENT
US Olympic Committee
DESIGN FIRM
Landor Associates
DESIGNERS
Tina Schoepflin, Paul Chock,
Margaret Youngblood, Doug Biehn,
Meghan Gough

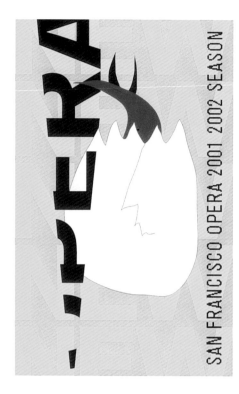

CLIENT
San Francisco Opera
DESIGN FIRM
Landor Associates
DESIGNERS
Alessio Krauss, Matteo Vianello,
Margaret Youngblood, Jonathan Fisher,
Doug Biehn, Caroline Yarker

SAN FRANCISCO OPERA
2002 2003 SEASON
BUILDING BRIDGES

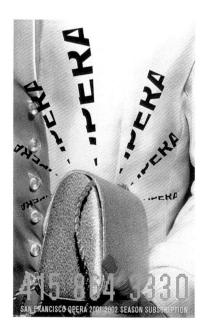

SAN FRANCISCO OPERA 2001 2002 SEASON

CLIENT
KAZI Beverage Company
DESIGN FIRM
Hornall Anderson Design Works, Inc.
DESIGNERS
Jack Anderson, Larry Anderson, Jay Hilburn
Kaye Farmer, Henry Yiu, Mary Chin Hutchison,
Sonja Max, Dorothee Soechting

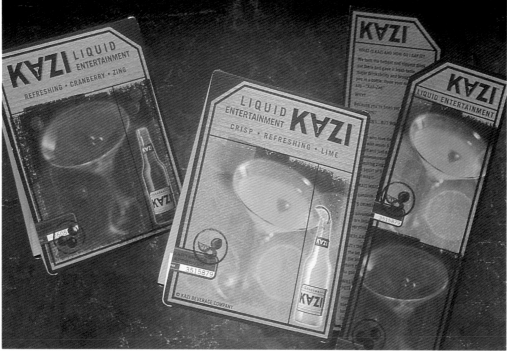

CLIENT
  Widmer Brothers
DESIGN FIRM
  Hornall Anderson Design Works, Inc.
DESIGNERS
  Jack Anderson, Larry Anderson,
  Bruce Stigler, Henry Yiu, Jay Hilburn,
  Kaye Farmer, Don Stayner

CLIENT
NCAA
DESIGN FIRM
Landor Associates
DESIGNERS
Kistina Wong, John Ledwith, Christopher Lehmann,
Margaret Youngblood, Jeff Jacobs, Meghan Gough,
Jennifer Jones, Tyler Mallison

CLIENT
Procter & Gamble
DESIGN FIRM
Landor Associates
DESIGNERS
Gaston Yagmourian, Christopher Lehmann,
Margaret Youngblood, Jonathan Fisher,
Phil Duncan, Meghan Gough, Rick Jansen

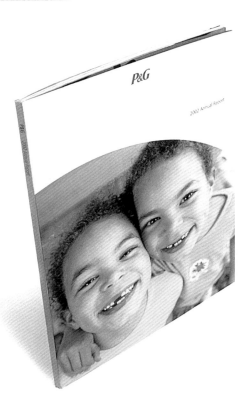

(1) Changing Consumer Expectations

CLIENT
Water•Color Inn
DESIGN FIRM
David Carter Design Assoc.
DESIGNERS
Donna Aldridge, Emily Huck

MEDIA GUIDE

AMERICAN LEAGUE
CENTRAL DIVISION CHAMPS

AMERICAN LEAGUE
CENTRAL DIVISION CHAMPS

SUITE POLICY
HANDBOOK

FAN INFORMATION
GUIDE

AMERICAN LEAGUE
CENTRAL DIVISION CHAMPS

CLEVELAND INDIANS

SEASON
SCHEDULE

CLIENT
  Cleveland Indians
DESIGN FIRM
  Herip Associates
DESIGNERS
  Walter M. Herip,
  John R. Menter

CAIRNS + ASSOCIATES

CLIENT
  Cairns + Associates
DESIGN FIRM
  Cairns + Associates
DESIGNER
  Ethan Ries

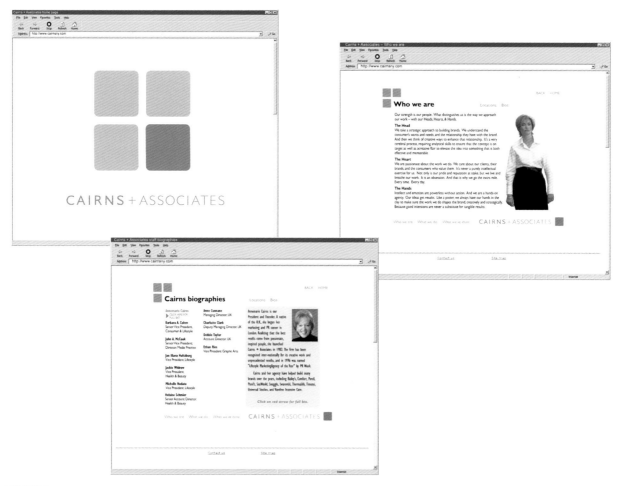

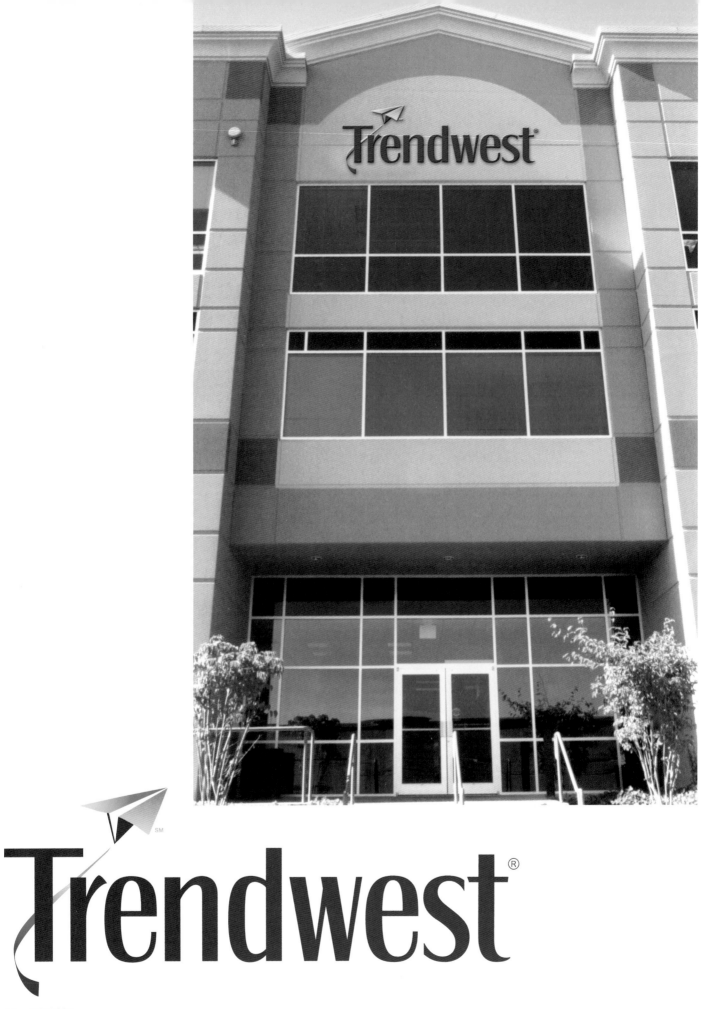

CLIENT
Trendwest
DESIGN FIRM
Walsh Design
DESIGNERS
**Miriam Lisco, Iskra Johnson,
Matt Wilson**

It all began with an idea.

Trendwest was founded in 1989 with two condominiums and a fresh idea. The idea was to combine a network of drive-to resorts with a flexible, point-based system of ownership. People liked it. Trendwest also created WorldMark to own and operate the resorts. And people loved it. At last they could afford to vacation—how, when and where they wanted. As a result, today Trendwest is a world leader in the vacation ownership industry, helping all kinds of people enjoy the benefits of the good life.

*Proof that dreams
really do come true.*

FOR INFORMATION ON HOW YOU CAN BECOME
A WORLDMARK OWNER, PLEASE CONTACT US

trendwest.com
productinfo@trendwestresorts.com
800-722-3487, ext. 2822

Trendwest®

Trendwest®

RESORTS

VACATIONS

YOU'RE GOING
SOMEPLACE FUN

Operational excellence.
Great assets and employees.

A clearly focused strategy

CenterPointEnergy.com

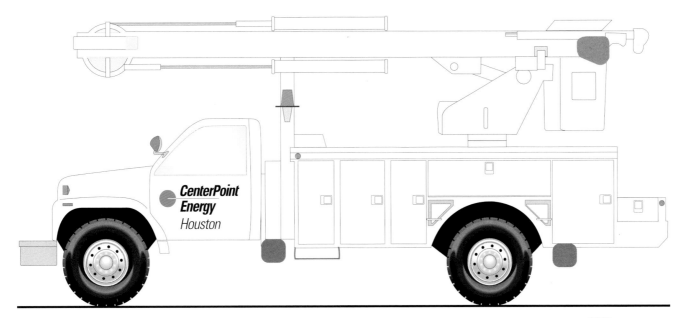

CLIENT
 CenterPoint Energy
DESIGN FIRM
 Lister Butler Consulting
DESIGNERS
 John Lister,
 William Davis

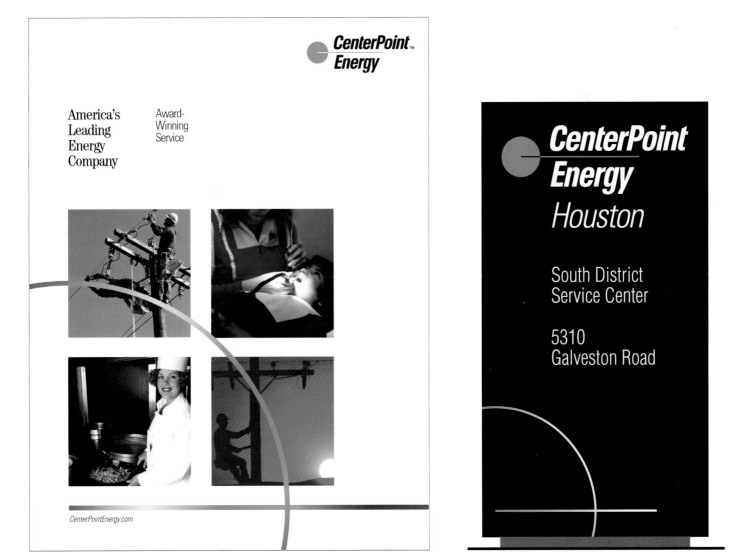

CLIENT
Royal Caribbean International
DESIGN FIRM
Brady Communications
DESIGNERS
Bryan Brunsell, Jim Bolander,
Phil Benner

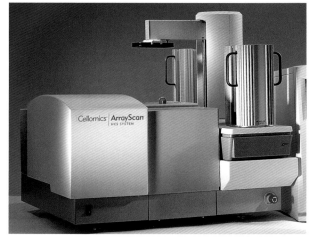

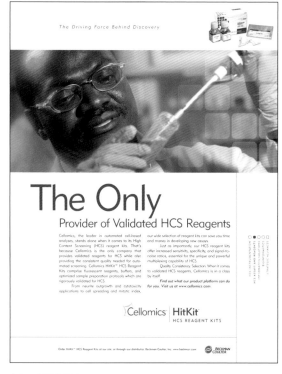

The Innovator
in Kinetic High Content Screening

Leave it to the leader in cell-based drug discovery to bring you an added dimension in High Content Screening.

The KineticScan™ HCS Reader is the first and only HCS screening system available that gives you the ability to measure drug-induced responses in live, individual cells over time.

Beyond its ability to provide environmental control and kinetic data, the KineticScan™ HCS Reader allows you to measure multiple factors, such as rate and reversibility — all with more enhanced capabilities and functionality than you ever thought possible.

If your success depends upon staying a step ahead, it's time to explore the possibilities of the KineticScan™ HCS Reader.

Find out what our product platform can do for you. Visit us at www.cellomics.com.

Cellomics | KineticScan
HCS READER

CLIENT
Cellomics
DESIGN FIRM
Brady Communications
DESIGNERS
Jim Bolander, Bryan Brunsell

CLIENT
  Hedstrom Corp.
DESIGN FIRM
  Brady Communications
DESIGNERS
  Bryan Brunsell, Jim Bolander,
  Dave Cameron, Matt Davis,
  Karen Lubinski, Jim Lilly

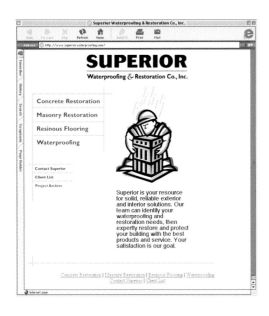

CLIENT
Superior Waterproofing
& Restoration
DESIGN FIRM
AKA Design, Inc.
DESIGNERS
John Ahearn,
Virginia Schneider

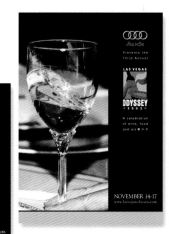

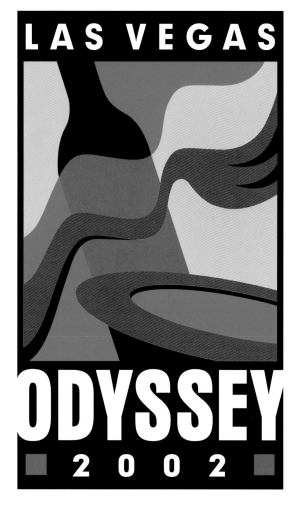

CLIENT
Las Vegas Odyssey 2002
DESIGN FIRM
Brand, Ltd.
DESIGNERS
**Virginia Thompson Martino,
Debbie Ketchum**

CLIENT
Renaissance Hollywood Hotel
DESIGN FIRM
David Carter Design Assoc.
DESIGNER
Donna Aldridge

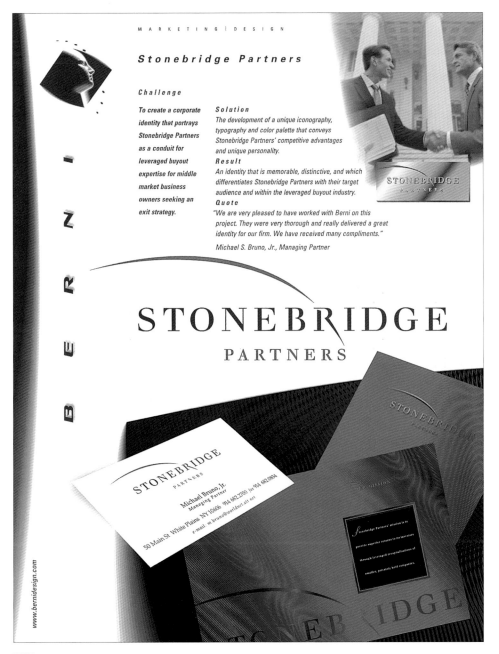

MARKETING | DESIGN

Stonebridge Partners

Challenge

To create a corporate identity that portrays Stonebridge Partners as a conduit for leveraged buyout expertise for middle market business owners seeking an exit strategy.

Solution
The development of a unique iconography, typography and color palette that conveys Stonebridge Partners' competitive advantages and unique personality.

Result
An identity that is memorable, distinctive, and which differentiates Stonebridge Partners with their target audience and within the leveraged buyout industry.

Quote
"We are very pleased to have worked with Berni on this project. They were very thorough and really delivered a great identity for our firm. We have received many compliments."

Michael S. Bruno, Jr., Managing Partner

STONEBRIDGE
PARTNERS

www.bernidesign.com

CLIENT
Stonebridge Partners
DESIGN FIRM
Berni Marketing & Design
DESIGNERS
Stuart M. Berni, Carlos Seminarlo,

CLIENT
Acappella Software
DESIGN FIRM
Berni Marketing & Design
DESIGNERS
Stuart M. Berni, Peter Antipas

Northstar

Challenge

To develop a leading-edge corporate identity for a new financial fund conveying an image of seasoned management and expertise

Solution
"Guiding star" graphics and logo created to impart experience and credibility; company positioned aggressively for asset gathering efforts.

Result
Immediately attracted desired target audience of investors ($500m). Established memorable image and perception in the minds of existing clients.

Quote
"Working with Berni on the unique Northstar logo has been a pleasure. We've received compliments from all our clients."

Mark Lipson
President/CEO

www.bernidesign.com

NORTHSTAR
NWNL NORTHSTAR FUNDS

CLIENT
NWNL Northstar Funds
DESIGN FIRM
Berni Marketing & Design
DESIGNERS
Stuart M. Berni, Mark Pinto

MARKETING / DESIGN

U.S. Smokeless

Challenge

Reposition 175-year old company to more closely align its corporate name with its consumer brands

Solution
Create a new name while leveraging equities of current heritage. Recreate brand image for the corporation under its revised eagle icon conveying innovation and leadership

Result
New corporate name and identity clearly support the new strategic plan

Quote
"Our new company name is a more accurate reflection of who we are -- the world's largest manufacturer and marketer of moist smokeless tobacco products"
Murray S. Kessler, President

UNITED STATES TOBACCO COMPANY
existing logo

www.bernidesign.com

B E R N I

CLIENT
USST
DESIGN FIRM
Berni Marketing & Design
DESIGNERS
Stuart M. Berni, Peter Antipas

PACKAGE DESIGNS

CLIENT
Bayer Consumer Care Division
DESIGN FIRM
Szylinski Associates Inc.
DESIGNERS
Ed Szylinski,
Frank Castaldi,
Stephan Shirack

CLIENT
Recreational Equipment, Inc.
DESIGN FIRM
Lemley Design Company
DESIGNERS
David Lemley, Yuri Shvets,
Matthew Loyd, Tobi Brown,
Jenny Hill

CLIENT
Vermont Pure Holdings, Inc.
DESIGN FIRM
The Imagination Company
DESIGNER
John Turner

CLIENT
Pedigree
DESIGN FIRM
Landor Associates
DESIGNERS
Andrew Otto, Heather Voelz,
Nicolas Aparicio, Rick Jansen,
Johanna Ramirez

CLIENT
Target Corporation
DESIGN FIRM
Target Corporation
DESIGNER
Angela Johansen

CLIENT
Twentieth Century Fox
DESIGN FIRM
Sargent & Berman
DESIGNERS
Peter Sargent, Barbara Chan,
Renee Pulve

CLIENT
Target Corporation
DESIGN FIRM
Target Advertising
DESIGNERS
Mike Rice,
Brad Hartmann

CLIENT
Target Corporation
DESIGN FIRM
Design Guys
DESIGNERS
Wendy Bonnstetter, Katie Kirk,
Steve Sikora, Karen Lokensgard

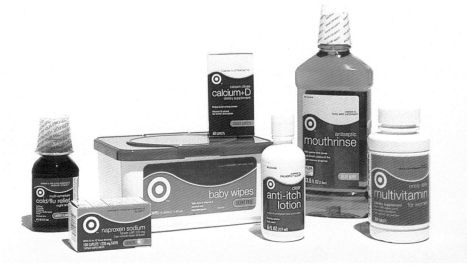

CLIENT
Target Corporation
DESIGN FIRM
Target Advertising
DESIGNERS
Ted Halbur,
Brad Hartmann

CLIENT
Tootsie Roll Industries
DESIGN FIRM
Cassata + Associates
DESIGNERS
James Wolfe,
Mary Holzer

CLIENT
Target Corporation
DESIGN FIRM
Design Guys
DESIGNERS
Jay Theige, Steve Sikora,
Jeanette Carrell

CLIENT
Onyx Hotel
DESIGN FIRM
Out Of The Box
DESIGNER
Rick Schneider

CLIENT
Teaology
DESIGN FIRM
Hornall Anderson Design Works, Inc.
DESIGNERS
Jana Nishi, Sonja Max,
Mary Chin Hutchison

CLIENT
ahold
DESIGN FIRM
Wallace Church, Inc.
DESIGNERS
Wendy Church, Stan Church,
Thorny Irrazaba

CLIENT
Nino Salvaggio
International Marketplace
DESIGN FIRM
Goldforest
DESIGNERS
Michael Gold, Lauren Gold,
Carolyn Rodi, Ray Garcia

CLIENT
Huffy Bicycle Company
DESIGN FIRM
VMA, Inc.
DESIGNERS
Rob Anspach, Al Hidalgo,
Joel Warneke

CLIENT
Breezy Garden
DESIGN FIRM
Mainframe Media & Design, LLC
DESIGNER
Lucinda Wei

CLIENT
Procter & Gamble
DESIGN FIRM
Lipson Alport Glass & Assoc.
DESIGNERS
Jen Voorhees,
Mary Jo Betz

CLIENT
Guinnes UDV
DESIGN FIRM
FutureBrand
DESIGNER
Diana Atkins

CLIENT
Target Corporation
DESIGN FIRM
Bamboo
DESIGNERS
Kathy Soranno,
Jeanette Carrell

CLIENT
Recreational Equipment, Inc.
DESIGN FIRM
Lemley Design Company
DESIGNERS
David Lemley, Yuri Shvets,
Matthew Loyd, Tobi Brown,
Jenny Hill

CLIENT
Target Corporation
DESIGN FIRM
Target Advertising
DESIGNERS
Cuc Oetting,
Jeanette Carrell

CLIENT
Target Corporation
DESIGN FIRM
Target Corporation
DESIGNERS
Dan Weston,
William Hovard,
Lee Iley

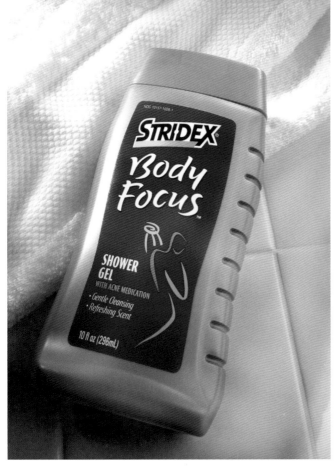

CLIENT
  Blistex, Inc.
DESIGN FIRM
  The Leyo Group, Inc.
DESIGNER
  Jayce Schmidt

CLIENT
  Prima Pharm
DESIGN FIRM
  Laura Coe Design Assoc.
DESIGNER
  Tracy Castle

CLIENT
  Humanitas Wines
DESIGN FIRM
  Deutsch Design Works
DESIGNERS
  Barry Deutsch,
  Larry Duke

CLIENT
  Zullo Communications
DESIGN FIRM
  Bonato Design
DESIGNERS
  Donna Bonato, Robin Bonato,
  Rebecca Uberti, Alison Scheel

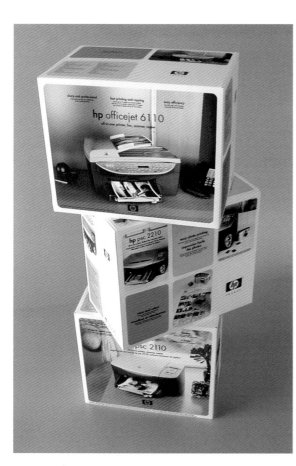

CLIENT
 Hewlett-Packard Co.
DESIGN FIRM
 Laura Coe Design Assoc.
DESIGNERS
 Tracy Castle,
 Thomas Richman

CLIENT
 Pepsi-Cola
DESIGN FIRM
 Deutsch Design Works
DESIGNERS
 Barry Deutsch, Eric Pino,
 Marion Schneider

CLIENT
 Diageo Caateau & Estate Wines
DESIGN FIRM
 Deutsch Design Works
DESIGNERS
 Barry Deutsch,
 Lori Wynn

CLIENT
 Anheuser—Busch Image Development
DESIGN FIRM
 Deutsch Design Works
DESIGNERS
 Barry Deutsch, John Marota

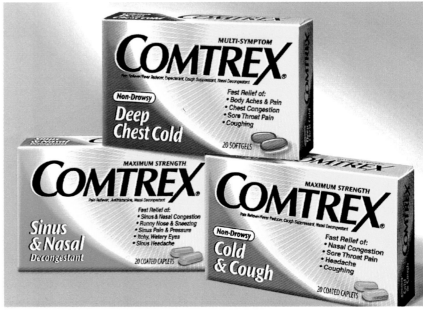

CLIENT
Bristol-Myers Squibb Co.
DESIGN FIRM
Hans Flink Design, Inc.
DESIGNERS
Susan Labodin,
Michael Carr

CLIENT
Snapple Beverage Group
DESIGN FIRM
FutureBrand
DESIGNERS
Joe Violante, Diana Atkins,
Chris Chevins

CLIENT
General Mills
DESIGN FIRM
Wallace Church, Inc.
DESIGNERS
Stan Church,
Jeremy Creighton,
Wendy Church

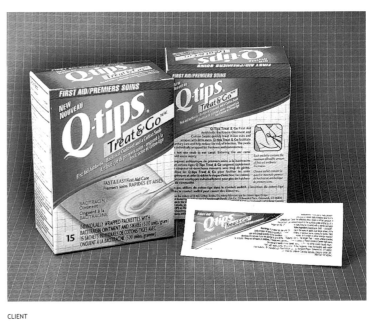

CLIENT
Unilever Home & Personal Care USA
DESIGN FIRM
Tom Fowler, Inc.
DESIGNERS
Elizabeth P. Ball,
Mary Ellen Butkus

CLIENT
Nestlé Purina PetCare Company
DESIGN FIRM
Thompson Design Group
DESIGNERS
Dennis Thompson,
Felicia Utomo

CLIENT
Recreational Equipment, Inc.
DESIGN FIRM
Lemley Design Company
DESIGNERS
David Lemley, Yuri Shvets,
Matthew Loyd, Tobi Brown,
Jenny Hill

CLIENT
GEDNEY
DESIGN FIRM
Compass Design
DESIGNERS
Mitch Lindgren, Tom Arthur
Bill Collins, Rich McGowen

CLIENT
Frito Lay
DESIGN FIRM
Landor Associates
DESIGNERS
Jon Weden, Hiroko Sudo,
Calvin Ng, Elly Donahue,
Danielle Pelczarski

CLIENT
Paul Mathews Vineyards
DESIGN FIRM
Buttitta Design
DESIGNERS
Patti Buttitta,
Lori Almeida

CLIENT
Canandaigua Wine Co.
DESIGN FIRM
McElveney & Palozzi Design Group
DESIGNERS
McElveney & Palozzi Design Group

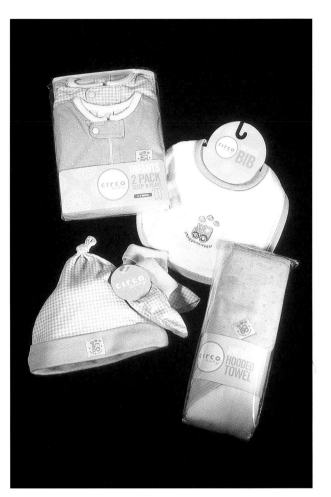

CLIENT
Target Corporation
DESIGN FIRM
Target Corporation
DESIGNER
Aaron Porvaznik

CLIENT
Federated Merchandising Group
DESIGN FIRM
Federated Marketing Services
DESIGNER
Anthony Ranieri

CLIENT
GM Hummer
DESIGN FIRM
Premier Communications Group
DESIGNERS
Randy Fossano,
Pete Pultz

CLIENT
International Foods & Confections, Inc.
DESIGN FIRM
Berry Design, Inc.
DESIGNERS
Bob Berry,
Yoon Lee

CLIENT
Fellowes
DESIGN FIRM
Steele
DESIGNERS
Scott Steele, Greg Steele,
Kyle Coss

CLIENT
Hipp O Records
DESIGN FIRM
Top Design Studio
DESIGNERS
Peleg Top,
Doug Prinzivalli

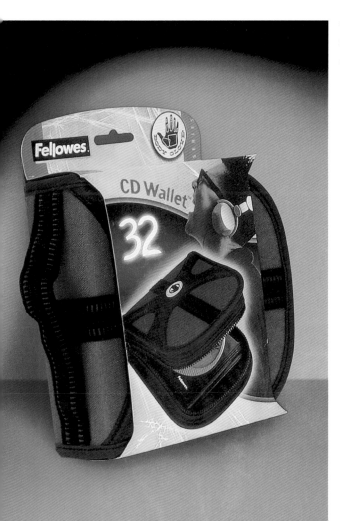

CLIENT
Coca-Cola Companies
DESIGN FIRM
Phoenix Design Works
DESIGNERS
Rod Ollerenshaw,
Darlene Pepper,
James M. Skiles

CLIENT
Canandaigua Wine
DESIGN FIRM
McElveney & Palozzi Design Group
DESIGNERS
McElveney & Palozzi Design Group

CLIENT
D'Arcy Cosmetics
DESIGN FIRM
Dula Image Group
DESIGNER
Michael Dula

CLIENT
Sony Computer-
Entertainment America
DESIGN FIRM
Creative Dynamics, Inc.
DESIGNERS
Eddie Roberts, Michelle Georgilas,
Victor Rodriguez

CLIENT
  ARL/Advanced Research Laboratories
DESIGN FIRM
  DiDonato Associates
DESIGNERS
  Peter DiDonato,
  Mike McGlothlin

CLIENT
  Frito Lay
DESIGN FIRM
  Landor Associates
DESIGNERS
  Jeanne Reimer, Hiroko Sudo,
  Jon Weden, Elly Donahue,
  Danielle Pelczarski

CLIENT
  Robinson Knife Company
DESIGN FIRM
  Michael Orr + Associates
DESIGNERS
  Michael R. Orr,
  Thomas Freeland

CLIENT
  Coca-Cola
DESIGN FIRM
  FutureBrand
DESIGNERS
  Kristen Juengst Donato,
  Laura Fang

CLIENT
New Line Home Entertainment
DESIGN FIRM
30sixty design, Inc.
DESIGNERS
Pär Larsson,
Duy Nguyen

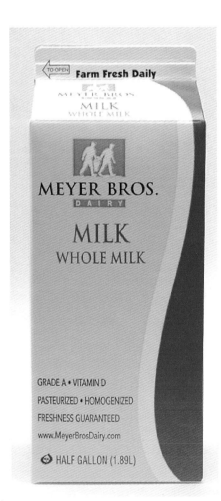

CLIENT
Meyer Bros.
DESIGN FIRM
Hillis Design
DESIGNERS
Anna Clark,
John Hillis

CLIENT
Betty Crocker
DESIGN FIRM
Compass Design
DESIGNERS
Mitch Lindgren, Bill Collins,
Tom Arthur, Matt McKee

CLIENT
Neohand
DESIGN FIRM
Brand, Ltd.
DESIGNERS
Virginia Thompson Martino,
Debbie Ketchum

CLIENT
Canandaigua Wine
DESIGN FIRM
McElveney & Palozzi Design Group
DESIGNER
John Westfall

CLIENT
Procter & Gamble
DESIGN FIRM
Interbrand Hulefeld
DESIGNER
Bart Laube

CLIENT
Sweet Blessings
DESIGN FIRM
Blinn Design
DESIGNER
K.C. Blinn

CLIENT
Hill's Pet Nutrition, Inc.
DESIGN FIRM
Zunda Design Group
DESIGNERS
Charles Zunda, Todd Nickel

CLIENT
Guiness Brewing Companies
DESIGN FIRM
Phoenix Design Works
DESIGNERS
James M. Skiles,
Rod Ollerenshaw,
Darlene Pepper

CLIENT
Batch Beverage
DESIGN FIRM
Out Of The Box
DESIGNER
Rick Schneider

CLIENT
Avery Dennison
DESIGN FIRM
FutureBrand
DESIGNERS
Jillian Mazzacano,
Rebecca Holtzman,
Ken Lewis

CLIENT
Frito Lay
DESIGN FIRM
Landor Associates
DESIGNERS
Hiroko Sudo, Margie Drechsel,
Jon Weden, Marco Ugolini,
Danielle Pelczarski

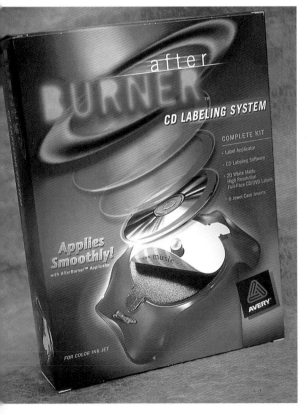

CLIENT
Target Corporation
DESIGN FIRM
Target Corporation
DESIGNER
Angela Johansen

CLIENT
Centage Corporation
DESIGN FIRM
Lee Busch Design Inc.
DESIGNER
Lee Busch

CLIENT
Skyy Spirits
DESIGN FIRM
Landor Associates
DESIGNERS
Anastasia Laksmi, Christopher Lehmann,
Nicolas Aparicio, Karolina Clevestig

CLIENT
Anitas
DESIGN FIRM
Schum & Associates
DESIGNERS
Guy Schum,
Scott Fowler

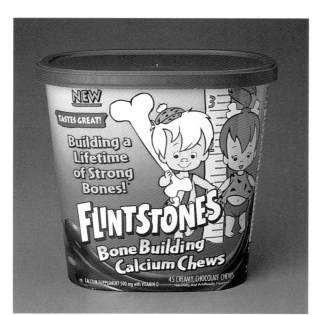

CLIENT
Bayer Consumer Care Division
DESIGN FIRM
Szylinski Associates Inc.
DESIGNER
Ed Szylinski

CLIENT
ClearBrook Farms
DESIGN FIRM
Lipson Alport Glass & Assoc.
DESIGNER
Mary Jo Betz,
Jay Bosse

CLIENT
S.C. Johnson & Sons, Inc.
DESIGN FIRM
The Weber Group, Inc.
DESIGNERS
Anthony Weber,
Martin Defatte

CLIENT
Nestlé Purina PetCare Company
DESIGN FIRM
Thompson Design Group
DESIGNERS
Dennis Thompson,
Patrick Fraser

CLIENT
Eastman Kodak Company
DESIGN FIRM
Forward branding & identity

CLIENT
Java City
DESIGN FIRM
Axion Design Inc.

CLIENT
Nestlé Purina PetCare Company
DESIGN FIRM
Thompson Design Group
DESIGNERS
Dennis Thompson,
Patrick Fraser,
Elizabeth Berta

CLIENT
Unilever HPC USA
DESIGN FIRM
Hans Flink Design, Inc.
DESIGNER
Shawn Bankston

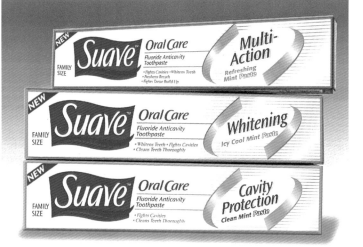

CLIENT
Sara Lee
DESIGN FIRM
Lipson Alport Glass & Assoc.
DESIGNER
Walter Perlowski

CLIENT
Procter & Gamble
DESIGN FIRM
Interbrand Hulefeld
DESIGNERS
Michael Palmer,
Christian Neidhard

CLIENT
General Mills
DESIGN FIRM
FutureBrand
DESIGNERS
Scott Fischer, Peter Chieffo

CLIENT
Mission Foods
DESIGN FIRM
Axion Design Inc.

CLIENT
Target Stores
DESIGN FIRM
Design Guys
DESIGNERS
Steven Sikora,
Jay Theige

CLIENT
OneWorld Challenge
DESIGN FIRM
Hornall Anderson Design Works, Inc.
DESIGNERS
Jack Anderson John Anicker,
Andrew Smith, Andrew Wicklund,
Mary Hermes, John Anderle

CLIENT
Frito Lay
DESIGN FIRM
Landor Associates
DESIGNERS
Koji Miyake, Simon Thorneycroft,
Elly Donahue, Danielle Pelczarski

CLIENT
Kroger
DESIGN FIRM
Interbrand Hulefeld
DESIGNER
Dennis Dill

CLIENT
Unilever Best Foods
DESIGN FIRM
Lipson Alport Glass & Assoc.
DESIGNERS
Mark Krukonis,
Walter Perlowski

CLIENT
Freemark Abbey
DESIGN FIRM
Thompson Design Group
DESIGNERS
Dennis Thompson,
Felicia Utomo

CLIENT
Kemps
DESIGN FIRM
Compass Design
DESIGNERS
Mitch Lindgren, Tom Arthur,
Rich McGowen

CLIENT
Kemps
DESIGN FIRM
Compass Design
DESIGNERS
Mitch Lindgren,
Tom Arthur,
Rich McGowen

CLIENT
Honyewell Consumer Products
DESIGN FIRM
Tom Fowler, Inc.
DESIGNERS
Mary Ellen Butkus,
Brien O'Reilly

CLIENT
Benz Family Vineyard
DESIGN FIRM
Mainframe Media & Design
DESIGNER
Lucinda Wei

CLIENT
Madre's Restaurant/Jennifer Lopez
DESIGN FIRM
EPOS, Inc.
DESIGNERS
Gabrielle Raumberger, Clifford Singontiko,
Chad M. Goodson, Eric "Sharky" Martinez,
Samantha Ahdoot, John Wersbe

CLIENT
Sticky Fingers Bakery
DESIGN FIRM
Hornall Anderson Design Works, Inc.
DESIGNERS
Jana Nishi, Henry Yiu

CLIENT
Pillsbury
DESIGN FIRM
FutureBrand
DESIGNERS
Scott Fischer,
Peter Chieffo

CLIENT
Kemps
DESIGN FIRM
Compass Design
DESIGNERS
Mitch Lindgren,
Tom Arthur,
Rich McGowen

CLIENT
DIDCO Imports Inc.
DESIGN FIRM
Susan Meshberg Graphic Design
DESIGNERS
Susan Meshberg,
Rob Johnson

CLIENT
Pinnacle Foods
DESIGN FIRM
Zunda Design Group
DESIGNERS
Charles Zunda, Todd Nickel

CLIENT
August Schell Brewing Co.
DESIGN FIRM
Compass Design
DESIGNERS
Mitch Lindgren, Tom Arthur,
Rich McGowen

CLIENT
Ventana Vineyards
DESIGN FIRM
Full Steam Marketing & Design
DESIGNERS
Lori Hughes,
Darryl Zimmerman

CLIENT
Black Rock Brewing
DESIGN FIRM
Out Of The Box
DESIGNER
Rick Schneider

CLIENT
Recreational Equipment, Inc.
DESIGN FIRM
Lemley Design Company
DESIGNERS
David Lemley, Yuri Shvets,
Matthew Loyd, Tobi Brown,
Jenny Hill

CLIENT
  McManis Family Vineyard
DESIGN FIRM
  Marcia Herrmann Design
DESIGNER
  Marcia Herrmann

CLIENT
  Snapple Beverage Group
DESIGN FIRM
  FutureBrand
DESIGNERS
  Chris Chevins,
  Joe Violante

CLIENT
  Pamela's Products
DESIGN FIRM
  Dickson Design
DESIGNER
  Deborah Shea

CLIENT
  Target Corporation
DESIGN FIRM
  Target Advertising
DESIGNERS
  Mike Rice, Brad Hartmann,
  Molly Zakrajsek

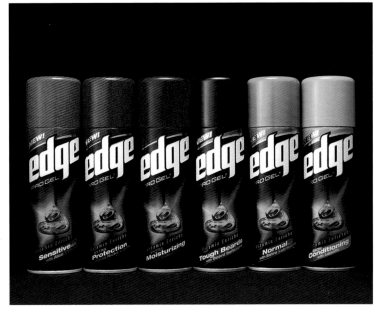

CLIENT
S.C. Johnson & Son, Inc.
DESIGN FIRM
The Weber Group, Inc.
DESIGNERS
Anthony Weber,
Scott Schreiber

CLIENT
Honyewell Consumer Products
DESIGN FIRM
Tom Fowler, Inc.
DESIGNERS
Mary Ellen Butkus,
Brien O'Reilly

CLIENT
Frito Lay
DESIGN FIRM
Landor Associates
DESIGNERS
Enzo Granella, Koji Miyake,
Simon Thorneycroft,
Michael Lamotte Studios
Elly Donahue, Danielle Pelczarski

CLIENT
Sun-Ni Cheese
DESIGN FIRM
Dean Design
DESIGNER
Jeff Phillips

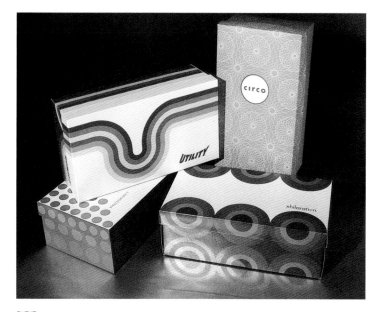

CLIENT
Target Corporation
DESIGN FIRM
Target Corporation
DESIGNERS
**Ron Anderson, Aaron Porvaznik,
Dan Weston, Kari Cook**

CLIENT
Widmer Brothers
DESIGN FIRM
Hornall Anderson Design Works, Inc.
DESIGNERS
**Jack Anderson, Larry Anderson,
Bruce Stigler, Jay Hilburn,
Henry Yiu, Kaye Farmer,
Don Stayner**

CLIENT
Target
DESIGN FIRM
Graphiculture
DESIGNERS
Sharon McKendry, Cheryl Watson

CLIENT
Gillette
DESIGN FIRM
Wallace Church, Inc.
DESIGNERS
**Stan Church,
David Minkley,
Jeremy Creighton**

CLIENT
August Schell Brewing Co.
DESIGN FIRM
Compass Design
DESIGNERS
Mitch Lindgren,
Tom Arthur,
Rich McGowen

CLIENT
William Grant and Sons
DESIGN FIRM
Bailey Design Group
DESIGNERS
Layne Lyons,
Steve Perry

CLIENT
Cadaco
DESIGN FIRM
Design Resource Center
DESIGNERS
John Norman,
Marc Rumaner

CLIENT
Kashi Company
DESIGN FIRM
Mark Oliver, Inc.
DESIGNER
Mark Oliver

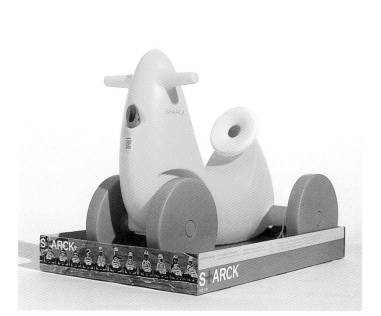

CLIENT
Ahold
DESIGN FIRM
Lipson Alport Glass & Assoc.
DESIGNERS
Claire Strykowski,
Christie McMearty,
Kara Fleming,
Scott Hardy

CLIENT
Target Stores
DESIGN FIRM
Design Guys
DESIGNERS
John Moes, Steve Sikora, Gary Patch,
Mark LaFavor, Mondino, Sara Johnson,
Maureen White, Eric Luoma, Lucy Winter

CLIENT
GoBoulder/RTD
(Regional Transportation Dist.)
DESIGN FIRM
CommArts
DESIGNER
David Tweed

CLIENT
Clayton's
DESIGN FIRM
Marcia Herrmann Design
DESIGNER
Marcia Herrmann

CLIENT
  Nestlé Purina PetCare Company
DESIGN FIRM
  Thompson Design Group
DESIGNERS
  Dennis Thompson,
  Dan Bishop,
  Trevor Thompson

CLIENT
  Heinz
DESIGN FIRM
  Lipson Alport Glass & Assoc.
DESIGNER
  Jamey Wagner

CLIENT
  Nordstrom
DESIGN FIRM
  Hornall Anderson Design Works, Inc.
DESIGNERS
  Jack Anderson, Debra McCloskey,
  Steffanie Lorig, Beckon Wyld,
  Andrew Wicklund

CLIENT
  Boehringer Ingelhiem
DESIGN FIRM
  Zunda Design Group
DESIGNERS
  Charles Zunda,
  Todd Nickel

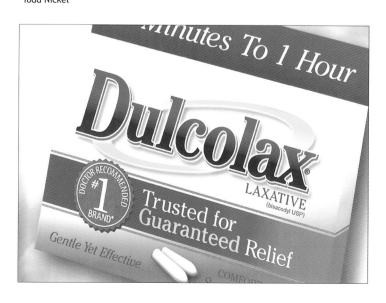

CLIENT
  Kensington Creative Worldwide, Inc.
DESIGN FIRM
  Kensington Creative Worldwide, Inc.
DESIGNERS
  Kensington Creative Worldwide, Inc.

CLIENT
  Grande Food
DESIGN FIRM
  Mark Oliver, Inc.
DESIGNER
  Mark Oliver

CLIENT
  Schering-Plough
DESIGN FIRM
  Lipson Alport Glass & Assoc.
DESIGNERS
  Mark Krukonis,
  Laurel Hanson

CLIENT
  Stellent
DESIGN FIRM
  McKnight Kurland Baccelli

CLIENT
  Target Corporation
DESIGN FIRM
  Design Guys
DESIGNERS
  Steve Sikora, John Moes, Gary Patch,
  Mark LaFavor, Jean Baptiste Mondino,
  Maureen White, Sara Johnson

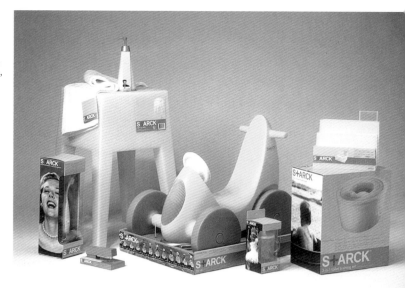

CLIENT
  Anheiser-Busch Image Development
DESIGN FIRM
  Deutsch Design Works
DESIGNERS
  Barry Deutsch,
  Eric Pino,
  John Marota

CLIENT
  Unilever Bestfoods
DESIGN FIRM
  Smith Design Associates
DESIGNERS
  Eileen Berezni,
  Lynn Vaughan

CLIENT
  Organic Milling
DESIGN FIRM
  Mark Oliver, Inc.
DESIGNER
  Mark Oliver

CLIENT
GoBoulder/RTD
(Regional Transportation Dist.)
DESIGN FIRM
CommArts
DESIGNER
Rachel Holt

CLIENT
General Mills
DESIGN FIRM
FutureBrand
DESIGNER
Scott Fischer

CLIENT
August Schell Brewing Co.
DESIGN FIRM
Compass Design
DESIGNERS
Mitch Lindgren,
Tom Arthur,
Rich McGowen

CLIENT
Target Corporation
DESIGN FIRM
Bamboo
DESIGNERS
Kathy Soranno,
Jenny Stevens,
Jeanette Carrell

CLIENT
Bellwether Farms
DESIGN FIRM
Mark Oliver, Inc.
DESIGNERS
Mark Oliver,
Patty Driskel

DESIGN FIRM
Capsule

CLIENT
Nino Salvaggio International
Market Place
DESIGN FIRM
Goldforest
DESIGNERS
Michael Gold, Lauren Gold,
Carolyn Rodi, Ray Garcia

CLIENT
Allied Domecq
DESIGN FIRM
Lipson Alport Glass & Assoc.
DESIGNER
Jamey Wagner

CLIENT
Arla Foods
DESIGN FIRM
Smith Design Associates
DESIGNER
Laura Markley

CLIENT
Wayne Imports, Inc.
DESIGN FIRM
Axion Design Inc.

CLIENT
Snapple Beverage Group
DESIGN FIRM
FutureBrand
DESIGNERS
Jillian Mazzacano,
Joe Violante

CLIENT
Good Humor-Breyers
DESIGN FIRM
Smith Design Associates
DESIGNER
Carol Konkowski

CLIENT
Recreational Equipment, Inc.
DESIGN FIRM
Lemley Design Company
DESIGNERS
David Lemley, Yuri Shvets,
Matthew Loyd, Tobi Brown,
Jenny Hill

CLIENT
International Foods & Confections, Inc.
DESIGN FIRM
Berry Design, Inc.
DESIGNERS
Bob Berry,
Yoon Lee

CLIENT
Unilever Best Foods
DESIGN FIRM
Lipson Alport Glass & Assoc.
DESIGNERS
Mark Krukonis,
Walter Perlowski

CLIENT
Kashi GoodFriends
DESIGN FIRM
Mark Oliver, Inc.
DESIGNERS
Mark Oliver,
Patty Driskel

CLIENT
  Creative Dynamics, Inc.
DESIGN FIRM
  Creative Dynamics, Inc.
DESIGNERS
  Michelle Georgilus,
  Mackenzie Walsh,
  Victor Rodriguez

CLIENT
  Wegmans Food Markets
DESIGN FIRM
  Forward branding & identity

CLIENT
  Skyy Spirits
DESIGN FIRM
  Landor Associates
DESIGNERS
  Kistina Wong, Anastasia Laksmi,
  Christopher Lehmann, Nicolas Aparicio,
  Karolina Clevestig

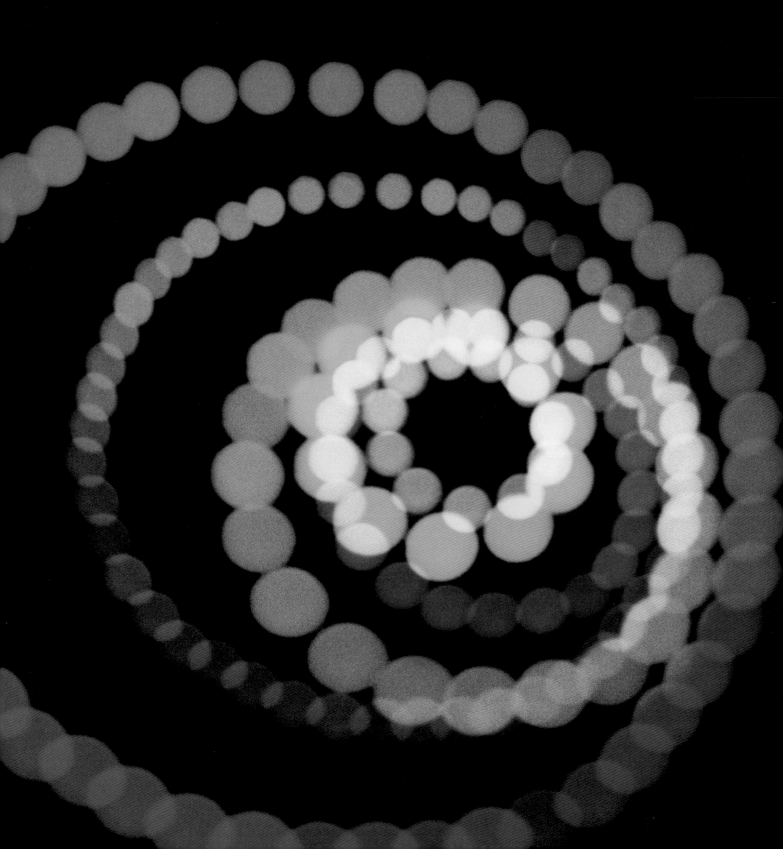

LETTERHEADS

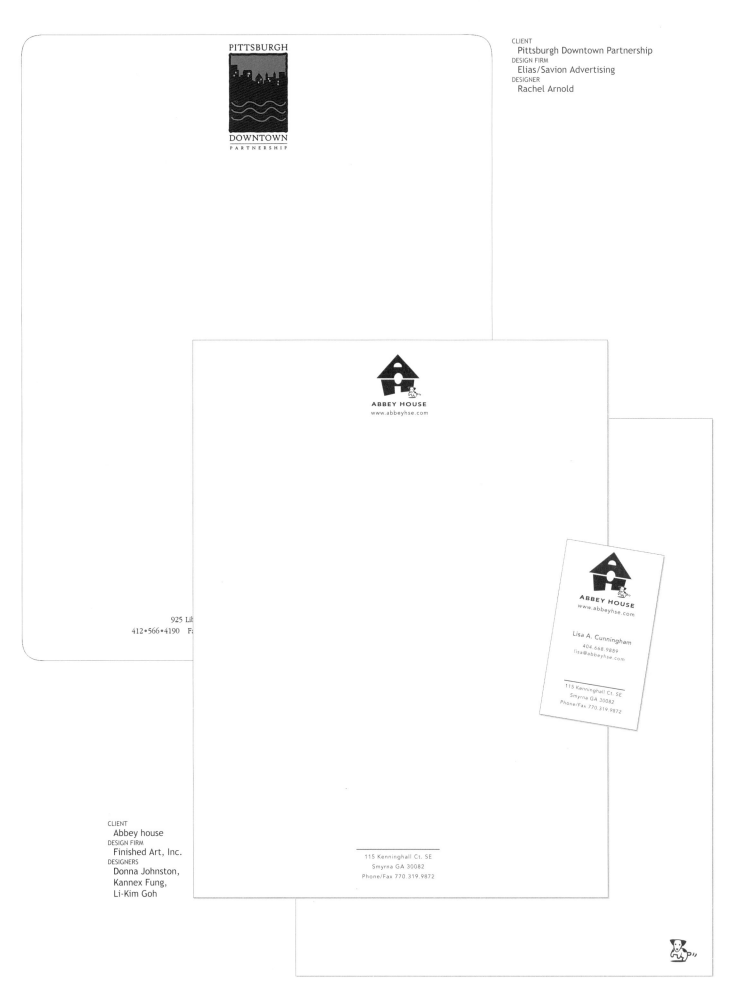

PITTSBURGH

DOWNTOWN
PARTNERSHIP

CLIENT
Pittsburgh Downtown Partnership
DESIGN FIRM
Elias/Savion Advertising
DESIGNER
Rachel Arnold

ABBEY HOUSE
www.abbeyhse.com

ABBEY HOUSE
www.abbeyhse.com

Lisa A. Cunningham
404.668.9889
lisa@abbeyhse.com

115 Kenninghall Ct. SE
Smyrna GA 30082
Phone/Fax 770.319.9872

925 Lib
412•566•4190   Fa

115 Kenninghall Ct. SE
Smyrna GA 30082
Phone/Fax 770.319.9872

CLIENT
Abbey house
DESIGN FIRM
Finished Art, Inc.
DESIGNERS
Donna Johnston,
Kannex Fung,
Li-Kim Goh

CLIENT
Unitus
DESIGN FIRM
Belyea
DESIGNERS
Ron Lars Hansen,
Naomi Murphy,
Anne Dougherty

tel 425.881.2264   fax 425.881.2085   P.O. Box 626 Redmond, WA 98073 USA   www.unitus.com

unitus

Rocio Urquijo   340 East 64th Street 9J New York NY 10021-7522

Telephone 212 371.7919 Telefax 212 371.7944

CLIENT
Rocio Urquijo
DESIGN FIRM
Nassar Design
DESIGNERS
Nelida Nassar,
Margarita Enconienda

1744 South Sherman Denver Colorado 80210 phone 303-715-4472 fax 720-294-0154

CLIENT
B Hawkins Inc.
DESIGN FIRM
Asher Studio
DESIGNER
Gretchen Wills

b hawkins inc

FIRST AMERICAN FUNDS™

P.O. Box 3011
Milwaukee, Wisconsin 53201-3011

800.677.FUND

www.firstamericanfunds.com

CLIENT
U.S. Bancorp Asset Management
DESIGN FIRM
Larsen Design + Interactive
DESIGNERS
Jo Davison, Todd Nesser

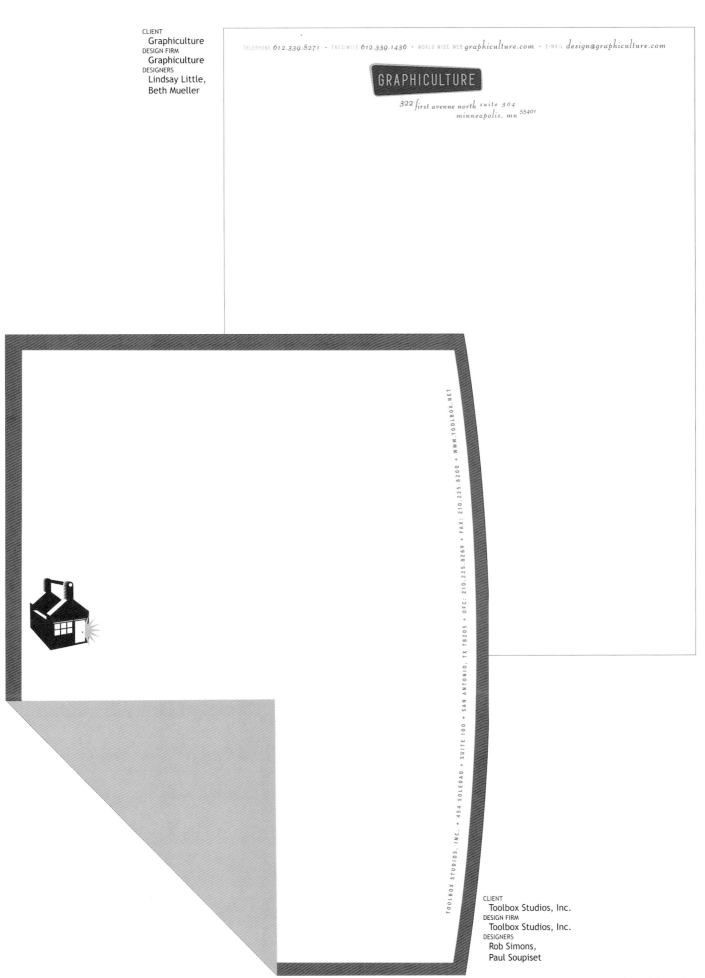

CLIENT
Graphiculture
DESIGN FIRM
Graphiculture
DESIGNERS
Lindsay Little,
Beth Mueller

TELEPHONE 612.339.8271 • FACSIMILE 612.339.1436 • WORLD WIDE WEB *graphiculture.com* • E-MAIL *design@graphiculture.com*

GRAPHICULTURE

322 first avenue north suite 304
minneapolis, mn 55401

TOOLBOX STUDIOS, INC. + 454 SOLEDAD + SUITE 100 + SAN ANTONIO, TX 78205 + OFC: 210.225.8269 + FAX: 210.225.8200 + WWW.TOOLBOX.NET

CLIENT
Toolbox Studios, Inc.
DESIGN FIRM
Toolbox Studios, Inc.
DESIGNERS
Rob Simons,
Paul Soupiset

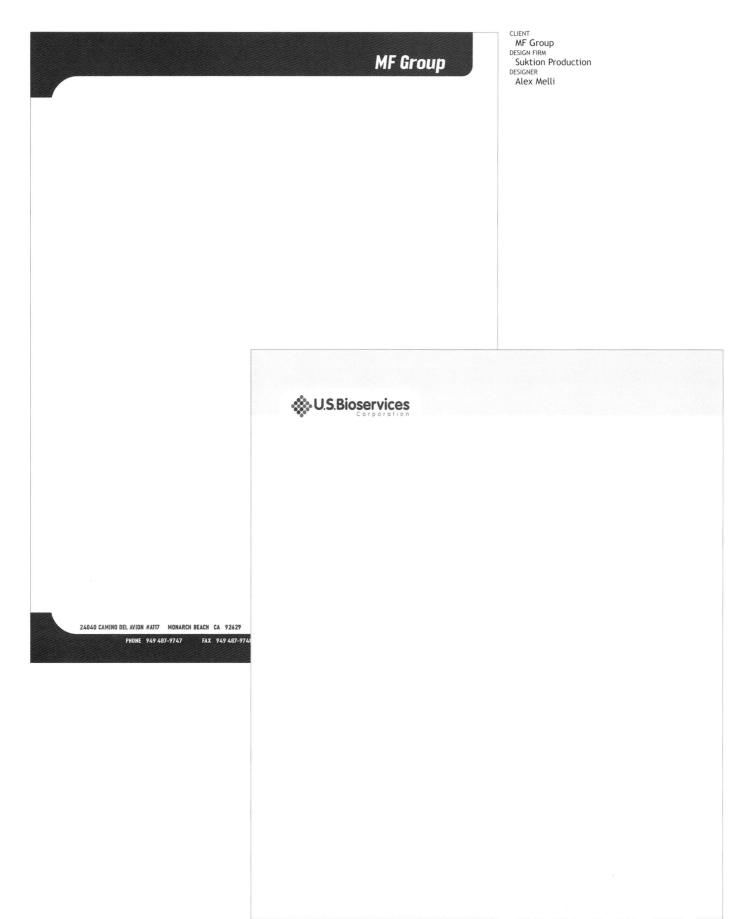

CLIENT
MF Group
DESIGN FIRM
Suktion Production
DESIGNER
Alex Melli

MF Group

24040 CAMINO DEL AVION #A117   MONARCH BEACH CA 92629

PHONE 949 487-9747   FAX 949 487-974

U.S.Bioservices
Corporation

2001 K Street, NW • Second Floor • Washington, DC 20006
P: 202.457.1900 • F: 202.828.2580 • www.usbioservices.com

CLIENT
U.S. Bioservices Corporation
DESIGN FIRM
Crosby Marketing Communications
DESIGNER
Tom Hight

KEEPING YOU ORGANIZED

CLIENT
Smead
DESIGN FIRM
Tilka Design

600 SMEAD BOULEVARD
HASTINGS, MN 55033-2219
p. 651 437 4111
f. 800 959 9134
www.smead.com

HASTINGS, MINNESOTA / LOGAN, OH

www.homeflashmedia.com

CLIENT
Home Flash Media
DESIGN FIRM
Indicia Design, Inc.
DESIGNERS
Ryan Hembree,
Cody Langford

100 Congress Center
100 Congress Avenue
Suite 2100
Austin, TX 78701

phone 512.469.6375
fax 512.469.3711

Promoting Brilliance, Inc

Unlocking the Power of People's Potential

CLIENT
Promoting Brilliance, Inc.
DESIGN FIRM
William Homan Design
DESIGNER
William Homan

hk
portfolio

hk portfolio
666 greenwich street
new york, new york 10014

telephone 212 675.5719
facsimile 212 675.6341

www.hkportfolio.com

CLIENT
HK Portfolio
DESIGN FIRM
Tilka Design

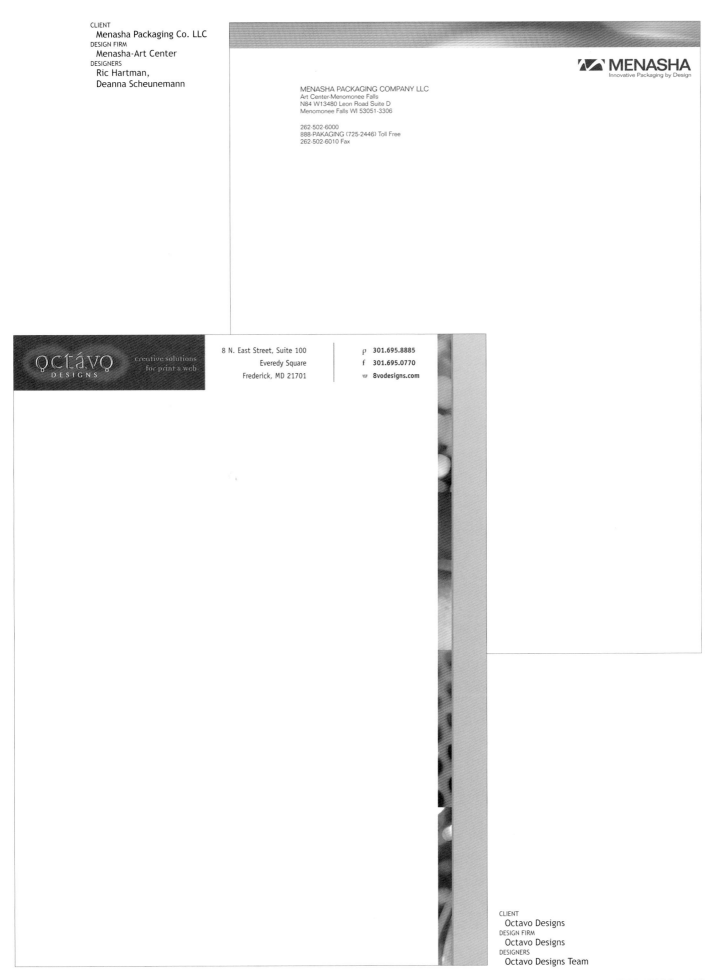

CLIENT
Menasha Packaging Co. LLC
DESIGN FIRM
Menasha-Art Center
DESIGNERS
Ric Hartman,
Deanna Scheunemann

MENASHA PACKAGING COMPANY LLC
Art Center-Menomonee Falls
N84 W13480 Leon Road Suite D
Menomonee Falls WI 53051-3306

262-502-6000
888-PAKAGING (725-2446) Toll Free
262-502-6010 Fax

MENASHA
Innovative Packaging by Design

octávo
DESIGNS
creative solutions
for print & web.

8 N. East Street, Suite 100
Everedy Square
Frederick, MD 21701

p 301.695.8885
f 301.695.0770
w 8vodesigns.com

CLIENT
Octavo Designs
DESIGN FIRM
Octavo Designs
DESIGNERS
Octavo Designs Team

HUBBUB
AN ADVERTISING AGENCY

158 NORTH GLASSELL
SUI

TEL 714.53
FAX 714.53

CLIENT
Hubbub Advertising
DESIGN FIRM
Hubbell Design Works
DESIGNER
Leighton Hubbell

St Stephen's   405 frederick avenue   sewickley, pa   15143   **t** 412.741.1790   **f** 412.741.7360   www.**ststephenschurch**.net

CLIENT
St. Stephen's
DESIGN FIRM
Sewickley Graphics
& Design, Inc.
DESIGNER
Michael Seidl

Out of the Box

Package Design
Brand Identity

215 Hanford Drive
Fairfield, CT 06824
P: 203.254.1437
F: 203.256.8055
Email: info@ootbdesign.com
www.ootbdesign.com

CLIENT
Out Of The Box
DESIGN FIRM
Out Of The Box
DESIGNER
Rick Schneider

KEPLER DESIGN GROUP
INTERIOR SPACE PLANNING
& DESIGN

256 LOS CERROS DRIVE
SAN LUIS OBISPO
CALIFORNIA 93405
V :: 805/594•1820
F :: 805/594•1821
E :: JK@KeplerDesign.com
W:: KeplerDesign.com

CLIENT
Kepler Design Group
DESIGN FIRM
Pandora + Company
DESIGNER
Pandora Nash-Karner

ZETTA LOU'S

HEAVENLY CATERING & POUNDCAKE FACTORY

204 NORTH WAVERLY STREET ~ ORANGE, CAL

AXION   smart creativity for brand success

MAIL PO Box 629 San Anselmo California 94979 PHONE 415.258.6800 FAX 415.459.6816 www.axiondesign.com

CLIENT
Zetta Lou's Catering
DESIGN FIRM
Hubbell Design Works
DESIGNER
Leighton Hubbell

CLIENT
Axion Design Inc.
DESIGN FIRM
Axion Design Inc.
DESIGNER
Ed Cristman

CLIENT
Western Payments Alliance
DESIGN FIRM
Kirshenbaum Communications
DESIGNER
Colin O'Neil

WESTERN
PAYMENTS ALLIANCE

www.wespay.org

APEX

apex search engine marketing   913 S. Lakewood Ave., Baltimore, MD 21224
p 410 342 1214 f 410 342 6341 1 800 324 1166

info@apexseo.com
www.apexseo.com

CLIENT
Apex SEO
DESIGN FIRM
re: salzman designs
DESIGNERS
Ida Cheinman,
Rick Salzman

CLIENT
Litecast
DESIGN FIRM
re: salzman designs
DESIGNERS
Ida Cheinman,
Rick Salzman

L I T E C A S T

Connect to Your Future

915 S. Lakewood Avenue
Baltimore, Maryland 21224

p 410 732 2756
f 443 267 0076

w.litecast.net ○ info@litecast.net ○ sales@litecast.net

CLIENT
American Diabetes Association
DESIGN FIRM
Adam Filippo & Associates
DESIGNERS
Robert Adam,
Martin Perez

CLIENT
Indicia Design, Inc.
DESIGN FIRM
Indicia Design, Inc.
DESIGNER
Cody Langford

INDICIA Design, Inc.

4149 Pennsylvania Ave.
Suite 203
Kansas City, MO 64111

816.531.3703 ph
816.531.3704 fax

www.indiciadesign.com

SUNAROMA®

CLIENT
Sunaroma
DESIGN FIRM
Mainframe Media & Design
DESIGNER
Lucinda Wei

MORROW ENGINEERING, INC.

6235 West Kellogg Drive | Wichita, Kansas 67209 | P: 316 9

CLIENT
Morrow Engineering, Inc.
DESIGN FIRM
Craghead & Harrold
DESIGNER
Shawn Stackey

WHERE WILL YOUR NEXT GREAT IDEA COME FROM?

ORIV●

PHONE
206.284.6646
FAX
206.691.3072

ADDRESS
19 W. Dravus Street
Seattle, WA 98119
URL
www.orivo.com

CLIENT
Orivo
DESIGN FIRM
Hornall Anderson Design Works, Inc.
DESIGNERS
Jack Anderson, Andrew Wicklund,
Henry Yiu

PRESSTECH

959 Lee Street
Des Plaines, Illinois 60016

P 847.824.4485
F 847.824.4775
E presstech@mc.net

◊ INK.

▯ PAPER.

♡ PRIDE.

CLIENT
  Presstech
DESIGN FIRM
  gripdesign
DESIGNERS
  Phil Truesdale,
  Kelly Kaminski,
  Kevin McConkey

702-269-2392 | VOICE
702-303-5649 | MOBILE
702-269-2391 | FAX

BARNEY

2535 SILVER BEACH DRIVE
HENDERSON NEVADA 89052

BARNEY
TABACH
ENTREPRENEUR

barney@lvcm.com

CLIENT
  Barney Tabach Entrepreneur
DESIGN FIRM
  Sayles Graphic Design
DESIGNERS
  John Sayles, Som Inthalangsy

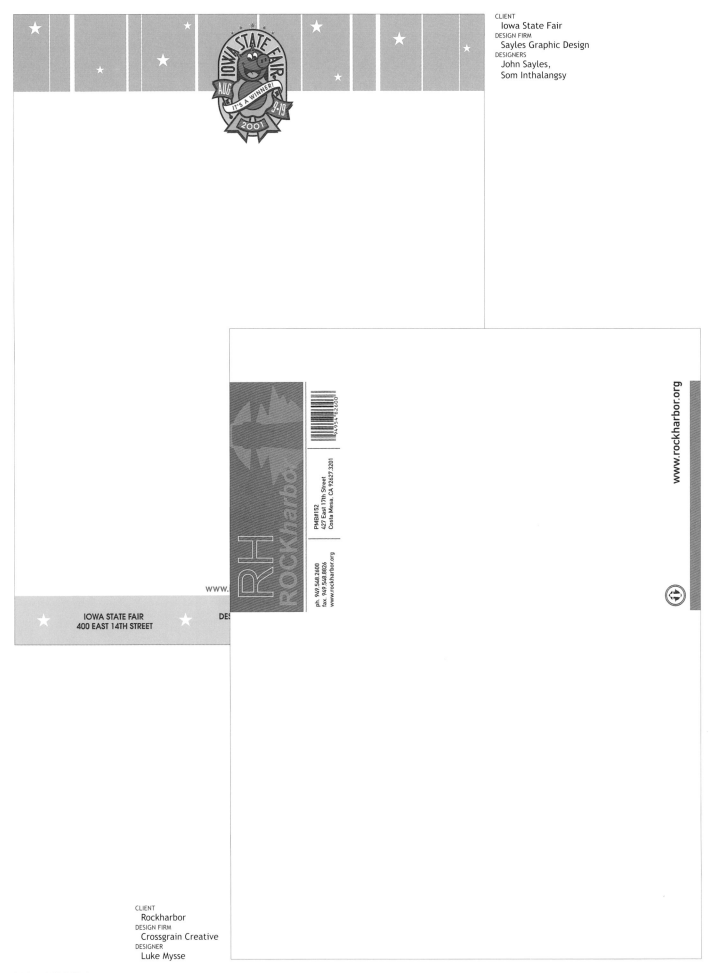

CLIENT
Iowa State Fair
DESIGN FIRM
Sayles Graphic Design
DESIGNERS
John Sayles,
Som Inthalangsy

IOWA STATE FAIR
400 EAST 14TH STREET

PMB#152
427 East 17th Street
Costa Mesa, CA 92627.3201

ph. 949.548.2600
fax. 949.548.8826
www.rockharbor.org

www.rockharbor.org

CLIENT
Rockharbor
DESIGN FIRM
Crossgrain Creative
DESIGNER
Luke Mysse

CLIENT
Mulvanny/G2 Architects
DESIGN FIRM
Hornall Anderson Design Works, Inc.
DESIGNERS
Jack Anderson, Katha Dalton,
Jana Nishi, Michael Brugman,
Henry Yiu, Hillary Radbill,
Ed Lee

MULVANNY G2

ARCHITECTURE

DESIGN AT WORK

12TH AVENUE NE | SUITE 500 | BELLEVUE, WA | 98004
annyG2.com

IN THE HUNT | CANINE ® EQUESTRIAN FARM

615.368.2443 PH
615.368.2444 FX
WWW.INTHEHUNTFARM.COM

8462 COVINGTON ROAD
EAGLEVILLE, TENNESSEE
37060

IN THE HUNT | CANINE ® EQUESTRIAN FARM

8462 COVINGTON ROAD
EAGLEVILLE, TENNESSEE
37060

615.368.2443 PH
615.368.2444 FX
WWW.INTHEHUNTFARM.COM

CLIENT
In The Hunt Farm
DESIGN FIRM
Hubbell Design Works
DESIGNER
Leighton Hubbell

mail_501 morrison road, columbus, oh. 43230
surf_www.prioritydesigns.com
call_614.337.9979
fax_614.337.9499

CLIENT
Priority Designs
DESIGN FIRM
Priority Designs
DESIGNERS
Paul Kolada, Sean Svendsen,
Chad Haas, Michael Painter

CLIENT
George Lepp + Associates
DESIGN FIRM
Pandora + Company
DESIGNER
Pandora Nash-Karner

GEORGE LEPP & ASSOCIATES

SHARING CREATIVITY

through professional

nature photography for

fine-art prints and

stock images.

SHARING KNOWLEDGE

through photographic

digital workshops,

seminars, journals,

and books.

PH: 805/528·7385

FX: 805/528·7387

www.LeppPhoto.com

P.O. Box 6240

Los Osos,

California

93412-6240

GOLDEN RETRIEVER RESCUE OF MICHIGAN

G R R O M
P.O. Box 250583
Franklin, MI 48025
Hotline 248.988.0154
www.grrom.com
kruchar@aol.com

CLIENT
Golden Retriever Rescue of Michigan
DESIGN FIRM
Lesniewicz Associates
DESIGNER
Amy Lesniewicz

MARCOZ
antiques • decorations

Boston Design Center
One Design Center Place
Suite 328
Boston, MA 02210
617 357 · 0211

CLIENT
Marcoz Antiques & Decorations
DESIGN FIRM
Nassar Design
DESIGNERS
Nelida Nassar, Margarita Enconienda

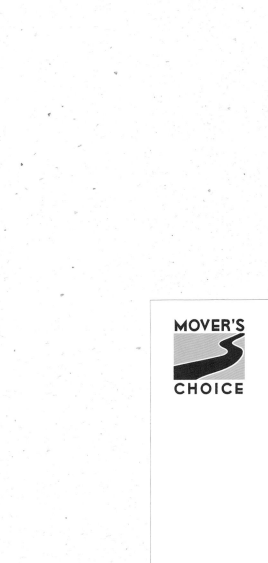

CLIENT
Planet Jupiter
DESIGN FIRM
Dula Image Group
DESIGNER
Michael Dula

PLANET
JUPITER

MOVER'S
CHOICE

1827 Clay Street
Napa, CA 94559
1-800-852-1968
707-252-5905 fax
moverschoice@paulhanson.com
www.paulhanson.com
License # OB64567

Packed and Delivered by Paul Hanson Insurance Services

CLIENT
Paul Hanson Insurance Services
DESIGN FIRM
Design Solutions
DESIGNER
Deborah Mitchell

Women's Care
PHYSICIANS & SURGEONS

Cristin Babcock, MD
Frederick Green, MD
Robert Jacobson, MD
Paula Jewett, MD
Gary LeClair, MD
Tina Schnapper, MD
Susan Trezona, CNM

598 E. 13th Avenue
Eugene, OR 97401
phone 541.342.8550
fax 541.485.7392

Douglas Austin, MD
Paul Kaplan, MD
Jeannie Merrick, NP

590 Country Club Pkwy.
Suite A
Eugene, OR 97401
phone 541.683.1559
fax 541.683.1709

Melissa Edwards, MD
Peter Hatfield, MD
Matthew Haugen, MD
Jennifer Tufariello, MD
Heather York, MD
John York, MD
Susan Armstrong, CNM

590 Country Club Pkwy.
Suite B
Eugene, OR 97401
phone 541.686.2922
fax 541.683.1709

Keith Balderston, MD
Vern Katz, MD

1200 Hilyard
Suite 570-S
Eugene, OR 97401
phone 541.349.7600
fax 541.686.8330

Deborah Dotters, MD
Audrey Garrett, MD

1200 Hilyard
Suite 570-S
Eugene, OR 97401
phone 541.465.3300
fax 541.686.8330

Karen Rutan, Administrator
phone 541.686.4194

CLIENT
Women's Care Physicians & Surgeons
DESIGN FIRM
Funk/Levis & Associates
DESIGNERS
Beverly Soasey,
Lada Korol

Wirestone 815 Park Boulevard, Suite 350, Boise, ID 83712 phone 208.343.2868 fax 208.343.1336 www.wirestone.com

wirestone

CLIENT
Wirestone
DESIGN FIRM
Dula Image Group
DESIGNER
Michael Dula

CLIENT
Frisbie Architects, Inc.
DESIGN FIRM
Resco Print Graphics
DESIGNER
Sandy Plank

We Create Design Solutions that Work!

F·R·I·S·B·I·E
ARCHITECTS, INC

215 N. Second St., Suite 204 | River Falls, WI 54022

TELEPHONE | 715.426.4908 FAX | 715.426.5886 WEB |

MeDiTecH
HEALTH SERVICES, INC.
The Personal Touch Professionals®

4562 Westinghouse Street, Suite A Ventura, CA 93003   800.538.0900   www.meditechhealth.com

CLIENT
Meditech Health Services, Inc.
DESIGN FIRM
Barbara Brown Marketing & Design
DESIGNERS
Barbara Brown, Jon A. Leslie

CLIENT
Southwest Restaurant Management Inc.
DESIGN FIRM
Ellen Bruss Design Team
DESIGNERS
Ellen Bruss, Charles Carpenter

**Funk/Levis
& Associates**

1045 Willamette St.
Eugene, OR 97401
EUG 541.485.1932
PDX 503.286.1095
FAX 541.485.3460

CLIENT
Funk/Levis & Associates
DESIGN FIRM
Funk/Levis & Associates
DESIGNER
Alex Wijnen

genoa
healthcare

CLIENT
Genoa Healthcare
DESIGN FIRM
Monster Design
DESIGNER
Hannah Wygal

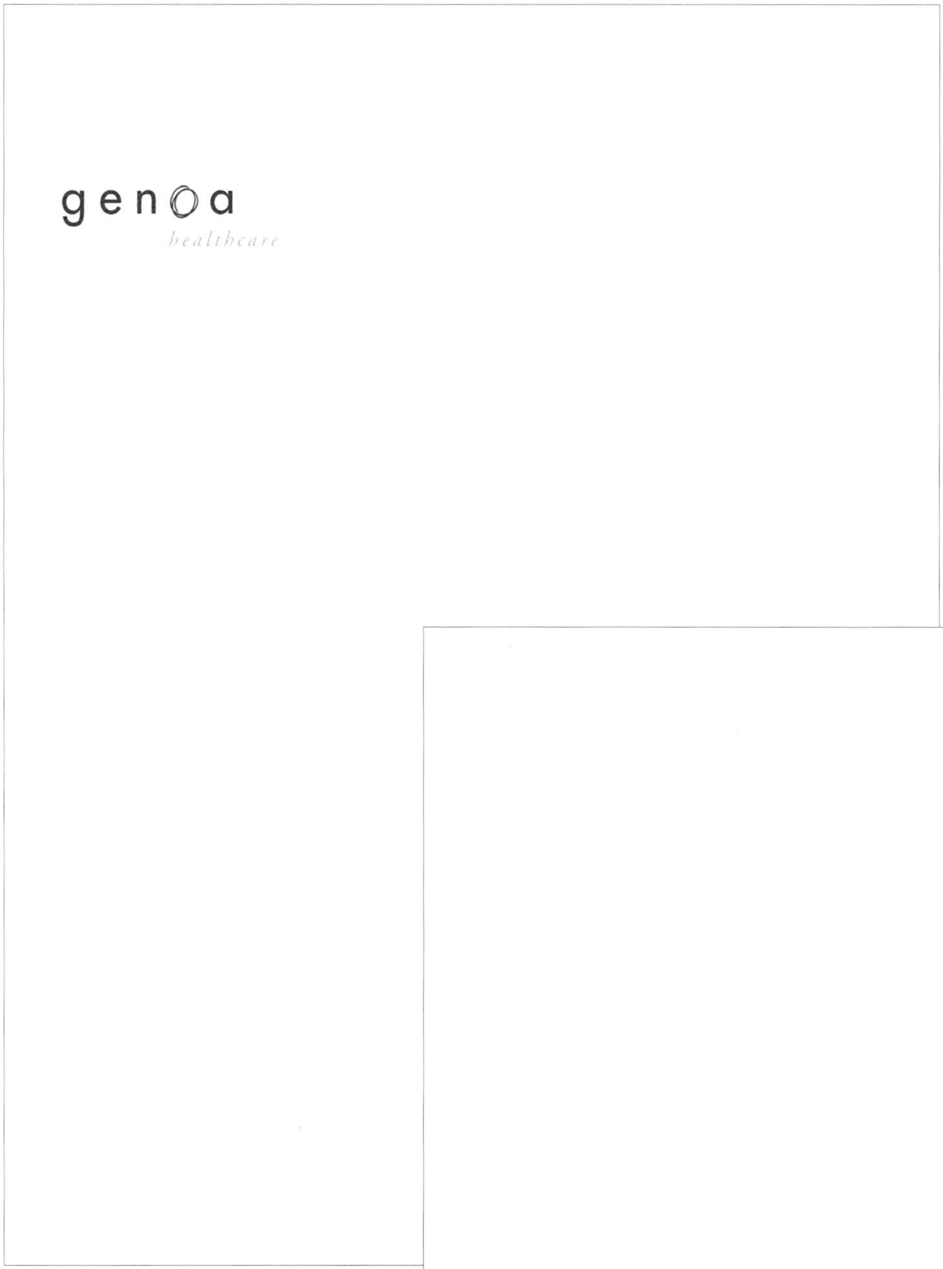

IMA

INDIANAPOLIS MUSEUM OF ART

4000 Michigan Road
Indianapolis, Indiana 46208-3326
Tel 317-923-1331 **Fax** 317-931-1978
www.ima-art.org

INDIANAPOLIS MUSEUM OF ART   VIRGINIA B. FAIRBANKS ART & NATURE PARK   OLDFIELDS–LILLY HOUSE & GARDENS

CLIENT
Indianapolis Museum of Art
DESIGN FIRM
Pressley Jacobs
DESIGNER
Jay Austin

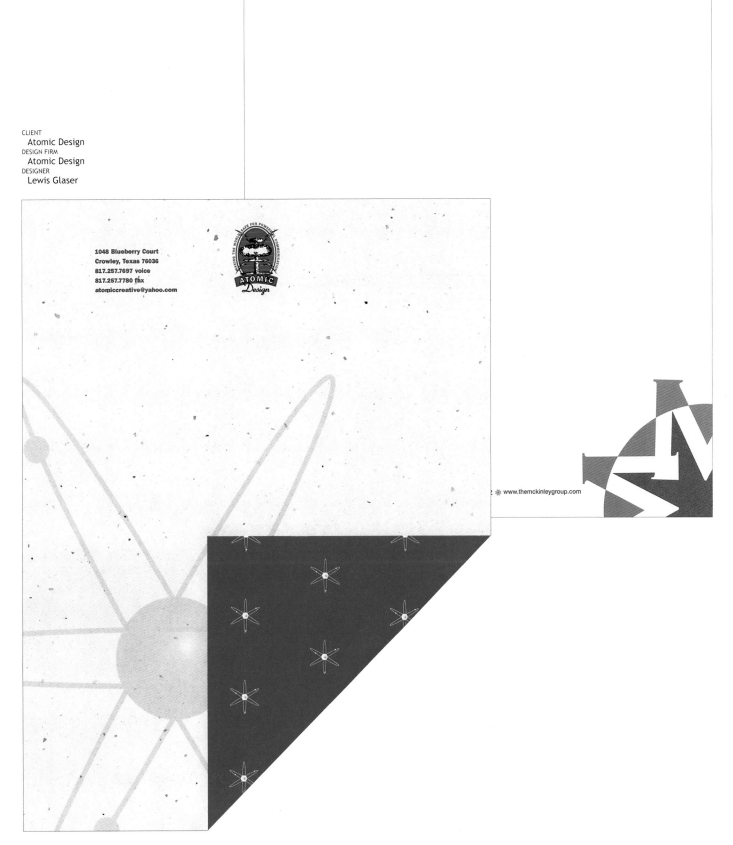

1048 Blueberry Court
Crowley, Texas 76036
817.257.7697 voice
817.257.7780 fax
atomiccreative@yahoo.com

www.themckinleygroup.com

CLIENT
Lonnie Duka Photography
DESIGN FIRM
Dula Image Group
DESIGNER
Michael Dula

LONNIE DUKA
PHOTOGRAPHY

352 THIRD STREET
SUITE NUMBER 304
LAGUNA BEACH
CALIFORNIA 92651
TEL 714 494 7057
FAX 714 697 2236

SAN
DIEGO
EYE
CENTER

RICHARD J. LEUNG, M.D.
*Laser Vision Correction Specialist
Diplomate, American Board
of Ophthalmology*

8008 Frost Street
Suite 407
San Diego, CA 92123
619.278.9900 *phone*
619.278.9984 *fax*

CLIENT
San Diego Eye Center
DESIGN FIRM
Hetz Advertising
DESIGNER
Michael Hetz

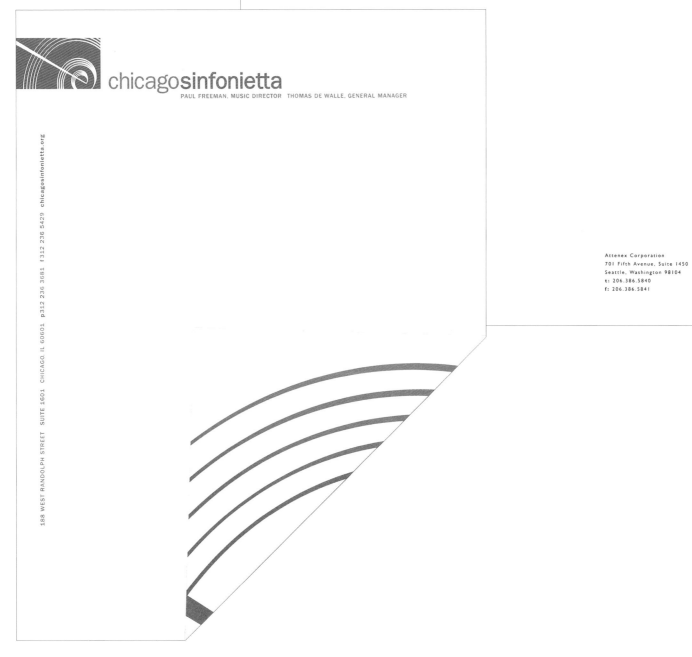

chicago**sinfonietta**
PAUL FREEMAN, MUSIC DIRECTOR   THOMAS DE WALLE, GENERAL MANAGER

188 WEST RANDOLPH STREET   SUITE 1601   CHICAGO, IL 60601   p312 236 3681   f312 236 5429   chicagosinfonietta.org

Attenex Corporation
701 Fifth Avenue, Suite 1450
Seattle, Washington 98104
t: 206.386.5840
f: 206.386.5841

CLIENT
El Dorado Park Church
DESIGN FIRM
Crossgrain Creative
DESIGNERS
Luke Mysse,
Rick Mysse

El Dorado Park
COMMUNITY CHURCH

ERICK§ON·McGOVERN
Architecture · Analysis · School Design

Erickson • McGovern, PLLC
120 131st Street S
Tacoma, WA
98444 - 4804
tel 253-531-0206
fax 253-531-9197

3655 NORWALK BLVD.
LONG BEACH, CA 90808
www.parkchurch.org

John Erickson	Rick McGovern	Steve Storaasli	Jay Peterson	Tzzy Wong	Gerry Pless
AIA, Partner	AIA, Partner	AIA, Partner	AIA, Partner	AIA, Partner	AIA, Associate

CLIENT
Erickson McGovern
DESIGN FIRM
Hornall Anderson Design Works
DESIGNERS
Jack Anderson, Kathy Saito,
Henry Yiu

CLIENT
Marcelo Coelho Photography
DESIGN FIRM
Top Design Studio
DESIGNERS
Peleg Top,
Rebekah Beaton

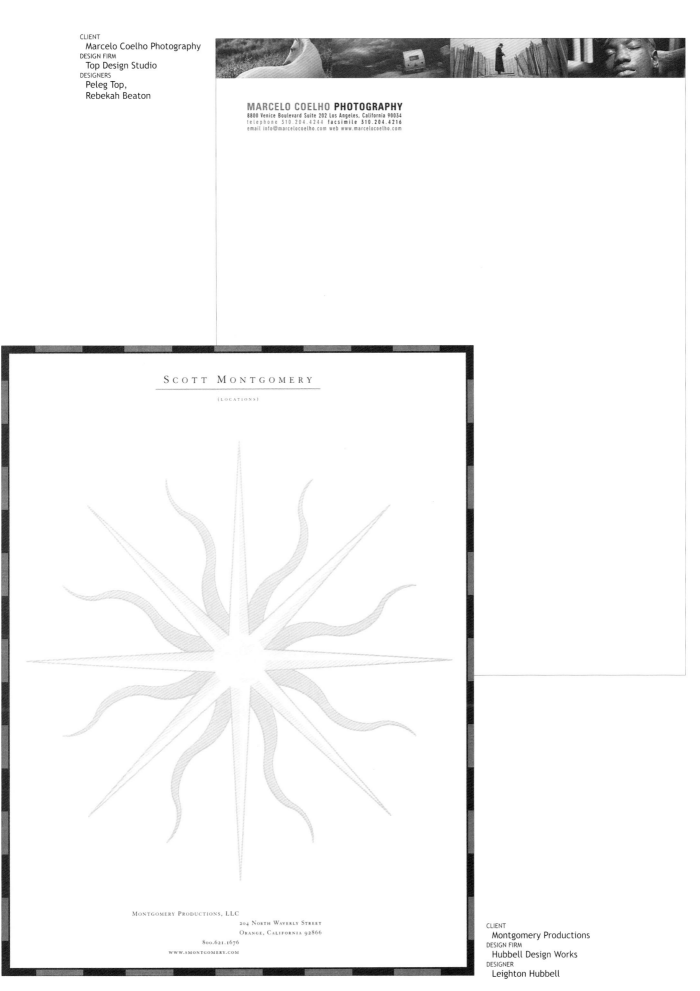

MARCELO COELHO PHOTOGRAPHY
8800 Venice Boulevard Suite 202 Los Angeles, California 90034
telephone 310.204.4244 facsimile 310.204.4216
email info@marcelocoelho.com web www.marcelocoelho.com

SCOTT MONTGOMERY

(LOCATIONS)

MONTGOMERY PRODUCTIONS, LLC
204 NORTH WAVERLY STREET
ORANGE, CALIFORNIA 92866

800.621.1676

WWW.SMONTGOMERY.COM

CLIENT
Montgomery Productions
DESIGN FIRM
Hubbell Design Works
DESIGNER
Leighton Hubbell

www.pictureplaneimaging.com   Telephone 310 393 0023   1316 3rd St. Promenade Suite 111
                               Fax 310 458 4881   Santa Monica, CA 90401

PicturePlane™
IMAGING SOLUTIONS

CLIENT
  Picture Plane Imaging
DESIGN FIRM
  Hamagami/Carroll
DESIGNER
  Jane Kim

NEXT YEAR'S NEWS, INC

COMMUNICATION: / WHATEVER IT TAKES!™

P: 419 241 3698 • 800 659 3615 / F: 419 241 3640 / WWW.NYNINC.COM
DELIVERY: ONE SOUTH SAINT CLAIR STREET • TOLEDO, OHIO 43602 / MAILING: PO BOX 907 • TOLEDO, OHIO 43697-0907

CLIENT
  Next Year's News, Inc.
DESIGN FIRM
  Next Year's News, Inc.
DESIGNER
  Andrea Colón

CLIENT
FreeMotion
DESIGN FIRM
Hornall Anderson Design Works, Inc.
DESIGNERS
Jack Anderson, Kathy Saito,
Sonja Max, Henry Yiu, Alan Copeland

FREEMOTION FITNESS INC™

Tel 719.955.1100
Fax 719.955.1104
Toll Free 877.363.8449

1096 Elkton Drive, Ste. 600
Colorado Springs, Colorado
80907-3573

DELAWARE HOTELS

1723 Fairway Drive • Hudson, WI 54016 • 715.386.2889 • fax 715.386.2825
e-mail: delawarehotels@msn.com

CLIENT
Delaware Hotels
DESIGN FIRM
Resco Print Graphics
DESIGNER
Hattie Thornton

sweet rhythm

Phone 212.255.3626
Fax 212.255.3661

www.sweetrhythmny.com

88 Seventh Avenue South
New York, NY 10014

JAM Entertainment Group, LLC

Wend-Tyler™

WEND-TYLER WINERY, INC.
4001 BECKWITH ROAD • MODESTO, CA 95358 • OFFICE/FAX: 209.548.9094 • MOBILE: 209.765.8160 • WWW.WENDTYLERWINERY.COM

CLIENT
Sweet Rhythm
DESIGN FIRM
Schnider & Yoshina Ltd.
DESIGNER
Lesley Kunikis

CLIENT
Wend Tyler Winery
DESIGN FIRM
Marcia Herrmann Design
DESIGNER
Marcia Herrmann

James & Karin Ameika, Owners

2701 Ridge Pointe Drive

Jonesboro, AR 72404

Voice 870.802.3220

Fax 870.932.5463

E-Mail beans@KonaCloudCoffee.com

www.KonaCloudCoffee.com

"DRINK YOUR COFFEE

WITH GLADNESS, WITH

A JOYFUL HEART,

EMBIBE OF THE BEAN,

ENJOY THE MOMENT."

- KING KONA

130   TEL 702.646.9067   FAX 702.646.9087   www.aqueadesign.com

The essence of imagination.

CLIENT
  Wallace Church, Inc.
DESIGN FIRM
  Wallace Church, Inc.
DESIGNERS
  Stan Church, Nin Glaister,
  Lawrence Haggerty, Wendy Church

Wallace Church, Inc.
Strategic Brand Identity
330 East 48th Street
New York, NY 10017
T 212 755 2903
F 212 355 6872
www.wallacechurch.com

ROSA D'ORO
VINEYARDS

3155 MERRITT ROAD • KELSEYVILLE, CALIFORNIA 95451 • TEL/FAX 707 279 0483

CLIENT
  Rosa d'Oro Vineyards
DESIGN FIRM
  Buttitta Design
DESIGNERS
  Patti Buttitta,
  Lori Almeida

CLIENT
InterCapital Partners
DESIGN FIRM
Doerr Associates
DESIGNER
Brad Paulson

Ironwood
ON THE GREEN AT FERNCROFT

lage Road, Middleton, MA 01949
6 • TOLL FREE: 866.774.4766 • FAX: 978.774.4675
ww.ironwoodonthegreen.com

terCapital Partners, Ltd. Development

The Copper Beech Inn
Ivoryton, Connecticut

860-767-0330 • *Toll free:* 888-809-2056 • *Fax:* 860-767-7840 • *Email:* info@CopperBeechInn.com
46 Main Street, Ivoryton, Connecticut 06442 USA

CLIENT
The Copper Beech Inn
DESIGN FIRM
Primary Design, Inc.
DESIGNERS
Jules Epstein, Allison Davis

CLIENT
Digital Brand Expressions
DESIGN FIRM
Zoe Graphics
DESIGNERS
Kim Z. Waters,
Kathy Paganc

CΦMEDICUS

Box 187 • 301 North Harrison Street • Princeton,

3989 Central Ave. NE, Ste. 610, Columbia Heights, MN 55421 p: (763) 788-8755 f: (763) 788-8660 www.comedicus.com

CLIENT
Comedicus, Inc.
DESIGN FIRM
Arnold/Ostrom Advertising
DESIGNER
Jacqueline Hoopman

CLIENT
EPOS, Inc.
DESIGN FIRM
EPOS, Inc.
DESIGNERS
Gabrielle Raunberger,
Clifford Singontiko

E^{11}

EPOS | endless
1639 sixteenth street | santa

SCIOVOX INCORPORATED
123 PRINCE STREET NEW YORK, NY 10012
ph.212.598.9306   fx.212.777.0435
amac@sciovox.com   www.sciovox.com

SCIOVOX INCORPORATED
123 PRINCE STREET NEW YORK, NY 10012
ph.212.598.9306   fx.212.777.0435
amac@sciovox.com   www.sciovox.com

AMANDA MCCAULEY PRESIDENT

CLIENT
Sciovox, Inc.
DESIGNER
Amanda MacCauley

CLIENT
Vornado
DESIGN FIRM
Insight Design Communications
DESIGNER
Lea Carmichael

VORNADO
Air Circulation Systems, Inc.

415 East 13th Street | Andover, KS 67002-9313 ℗ 316-733-0035 | 1-800-297-0883 ℉ 316-733-1544 ⱳ www.vornado.com

THE INSTITUTE FOR THE PRESERVATION
OF BANNED BOOKS: 1933-1945

5339 STRATHMORE AVENUE ■ KENSINGTON, MD 20895-1160
TELEPHONE: 301-933-5195 ■ FACSIMILE: 301-949-1680
EMAIL: ivanms@comcast.net

CLIENT
IPBB
DESIGN FIRM
Lazarus Design
DESIGNER
Robin Lazarus-Berlin

CAPSULE

TEN SOUTH FIFTH STREET || SUITE 645 || MPLS, MN 55402 ||
www.CAPSULELAB.com || TEL 612-341-4525 || FAX 612-341-4577

CLIENT
Capsule
DESIGN FIRM
Capsule
DESIGNERS
Brian Adducci, Dan Baggenstoss,
Greg Brose

⊙ TARGET.
marketing

1000 nicollet mall
minneapolis, mn
55403

CLIENT
Target Corporation
DESIGN FIRM
Target Corporation
DESIGNERS
Ron Anderson,
Kari Cook

S0334

CLIENT
ICS
DESIGN FIRM
Marcia Herrmann Design
DESIGNER
Marcia Herrmann

Integrated Construction Services

209-656-0640
Fax: 209-669-6891
412 S. Tully Rd.
Turlock, CA 95380

909-279-5531
Fax: 909-279-5552
1325 Pico, Suite 104
Corona, CA 92881
License #776486

The Soaring Spirit

the soaring spirit, inc. 11255 highway 55 suite 120 plymouth, mn 55441
p)763.546.2100 f)763.546.2102 thesoaringspirit.com

CLIENT
The Soaring Spirit, Inc.
DESIGN FIRM
Arnold/Ostrom Advertising
DESIGNERS
Lara Albrecht, Jacqueline Hoopman

209-527-2600
FAX:209-527-2650
821 13TH STREET, SUITE A
MODESTO, CA 95354

EIDER

CLIENT
  Eider Property
DESIGN FIRM
  Marcia Herrmann Design
DESIGNER
  Marcia Herrmann

 resource

CLIENT
  Resource Graphic
DESIGN FIRM
  Pressley Jacobs
DESIGNER
  Sarah Lin

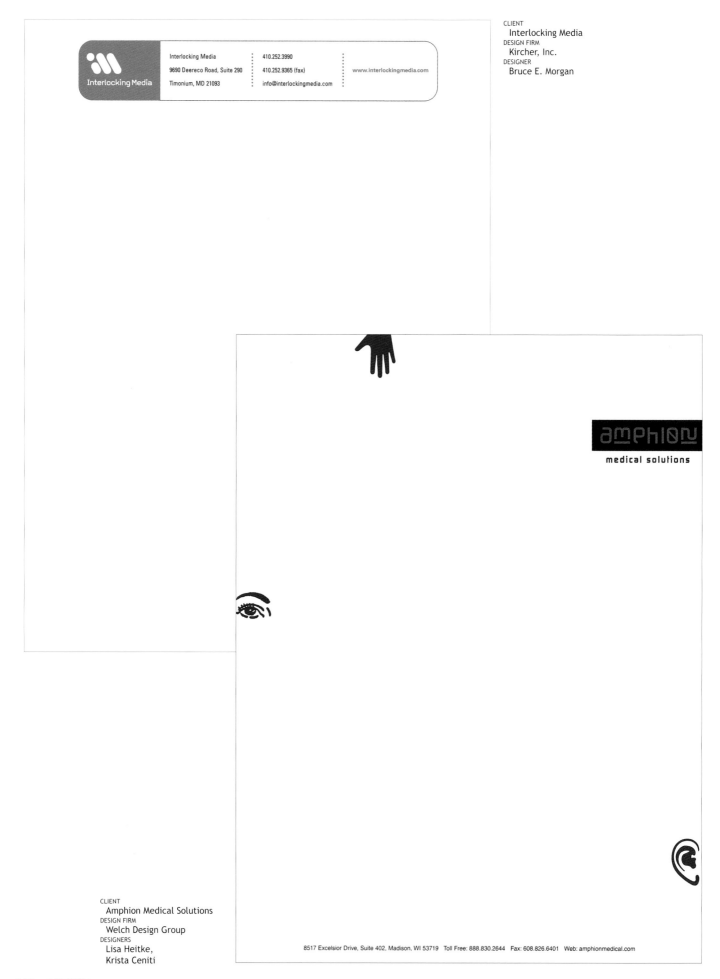

Interlocking Media

9690 Deereco Road, Suite 290

Timonium, MD 21093

410.252.3990

410.252.9365 (fax)

info@interlockingmedia.com

www.interlockingmedia.com

CLIENT
Interlocking Media
DESIGN FIRM
Kircher, Inc.
DESIGNER
Bruce E. Morgan

medical solutions

8517 Excelsior Drive, Suite 402, Madison, WI 53719   Toll Free: 888.830.2644   Fax: 608.826.6401   Web: amphionmedical.com

CLIENT
Amphion Medical Solutions
DESIGN FIRM
Welch Design Group
DESIGNERS
Lisa Heitke,
Krista Ceniti

D A V I D L A W **R E N C E** P H O T O **G** R A P H Y

136 GRAND STREET #4WF NEW YORK NY 10013 T 212 274 0710 F 212 274 0712 DALJR@AOL.COM

CLIENT
David Lawrence Photography
DESIGN FIRM
A + B
DESIGNERS
Alex Y. Suh,
Boyoung Lee

PACIFIC RACEWAYS
1100 NW LEARY WAY
SEATTLE, WA 98107

CLIENT
Pacific Raceways
DESIGN FIRM
Hornall Anderson Design Works, Inc.
DESIGNERS
Jack Anderson, Andrew Smith,
Sonja Max, Elmer dela Cruz, Ed Lee

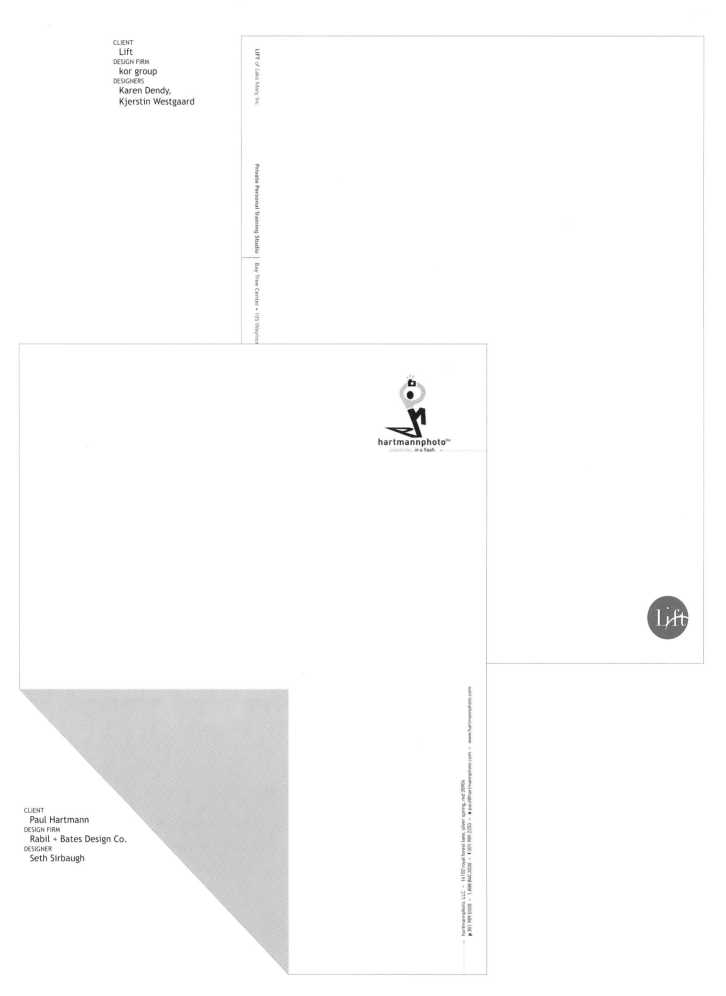

CLIENT
Lift
DESIGN FIRM
kor group
DESIGNERS
Karen Dendy,
Kjerstin Westgaard

LIFT of Lake Mary, Inc.

Private Personal Training Studio

Bay Tree Center • 105 Waymo

hartmannphoto llc
creativity...in a flash.

lift

hartmannphoto, LLC ► 14102 royal forest lane, silver spring, md 20904
p 301.989.0500 ► 1.888.840.3030 ► f 301.989.2253 ► e paul@hartmannphoto.com ► www.hartmannphoto.com

CLIENT
Paul Hartmann
DESIGN FIRM
Rabil + Bates Design Co.
DESIGNER
Seth Sirbaugh

CLIENT
A + B
DESIGN FIRM
A + B
DESIGNERS
Alex Y. Suh,
Boyoung Lee

A+B

TATE CAPITAL PARTNERS

PO Box 24499
Minneapolis, Minnesota 55424

UNG LEE
.com/ab.boyoung@yahoo.com

www.tatecapital.com

CLIENT
A + B
DESIGN FIRM
A + B
DESIGNERS
Alex Y. Suh,
Boyoung Lee

A+B

CLIENT
Tate Capital Partners
DESIGN FIRM
Larsen Design + Interactive
DESIGNER
Jo Davison, Bill Pflipsen

A NIGHT AT THE OPERA — ROCKFORD SYMPHONY ORCHESTRA'S **BLACK MAGIC 2002**

Christopher J. Laird,
Co-Chair

Robert Rhea,
Co-Chair

Linda Dennis
Greg Fedorev
B.J. Knez
Lisa Lindman
Betsey McCoy
Patrick O'Keefe
Rawley Rohan
Wendy Rubin
Scott Saporiti
Wendy Young

RIVERFRONT MUSEUM PARK, 711 NORTH MAIN STRE

PatchMail

PatchMail 3216 Pleasant Avenue South Minneapolis, Minnesota 55408

℡ 612. 824. 1156 🖶 612. 823. 0449 🖰 patchmail.com

CLIENT
Rockford Symphony Orchestra
DESIGN FIRM
Conflux Design
DESIGNER
Greg Fedorev

CLIENT
PatchMail
DESIGN FIRM
Larsen Design + Interactive
DESIGNER
Paul Wharton,
Todd Nesser

CLIENT
Michael Niblett Design
DESIGN FIRM
Michael Niblett Design
DESIGNER
Michael Niblett

1726 Hulen Street / Fort Worth, Texas 7610

LiesaHealy
Television Production
Multimedia Production
Media Training

t▸ 617-924-7740

c▸ 617-571-1020

e▸ liesa@liesahealy.com

w▸ www.liesahealy.com

CLIENT
Liesa Healy
DESIGN FIRM
CA Design
DESIGNER
Cheryl Allen

PROGRESSIVE
VITICULTURE   VINEYARD CONSULTING

OFFICE / FAX: 209-669-7656
CELL: 209-614-2565
P.O. BOX 2134
TURLOCK, CA 95381

CLIENT
  Progressive Viticulture
DESIGN FIRM
  Marcia Herrmann Design
DESIGNER
  Marcia Herrmann

H

HORNALL ANDERSON DESIGN WORKS

| TEL 206 467 5800 | FAX 206 467 6411 | hadw.com |

1008 Western Avenue, Suite 600
Seattle, WA 98104

CLIENT
  Hornall Anderson Design Works, Inc.
DESIGN FIRM
  Hornall Anderson Design Works, Inc.
DESIGNERS
  Jack Anderson, John Hornall,
  Henry Yiu, Andrew Wicklund,
  Mark Popich

CLIENT
Appleseed Healthcare Resources
DESIGN FIRM
Ken Cendrowski Design
DESIGNER
Ken Cendrowski

APPLESEED HEALTHCARE RESOURCES

Seeding efficiency in the delivery of care

Appleseed
837 Yorick Path · Wixom, Michigan 48
ehisscock@ap

DONNA BEST CLC
1011 2nd Street Suite 205 Santa Rosa, CA 95404
Tel 707 570 2041   Fax 707 570 2195

BEST

LIGHT   SPECIFICATION

CLIENT
d. Best Light Specification
DESIGN FIRM
Buttitta Design
DESIGNER
Patti Buttitta

CLIENT
InSite Works
DESIGN FIRM
Hornall Anderson Design Works, Inc.
DESIGNERS
Jack Anderson, Henry Yiu,
Kathy Saito, Sonja Max

Integrity in Design and Construction

CLIENT
Red Granite, LLC
DESIGN FIRM
Welch Design Group
DESIGNER
Krista Ceuiti

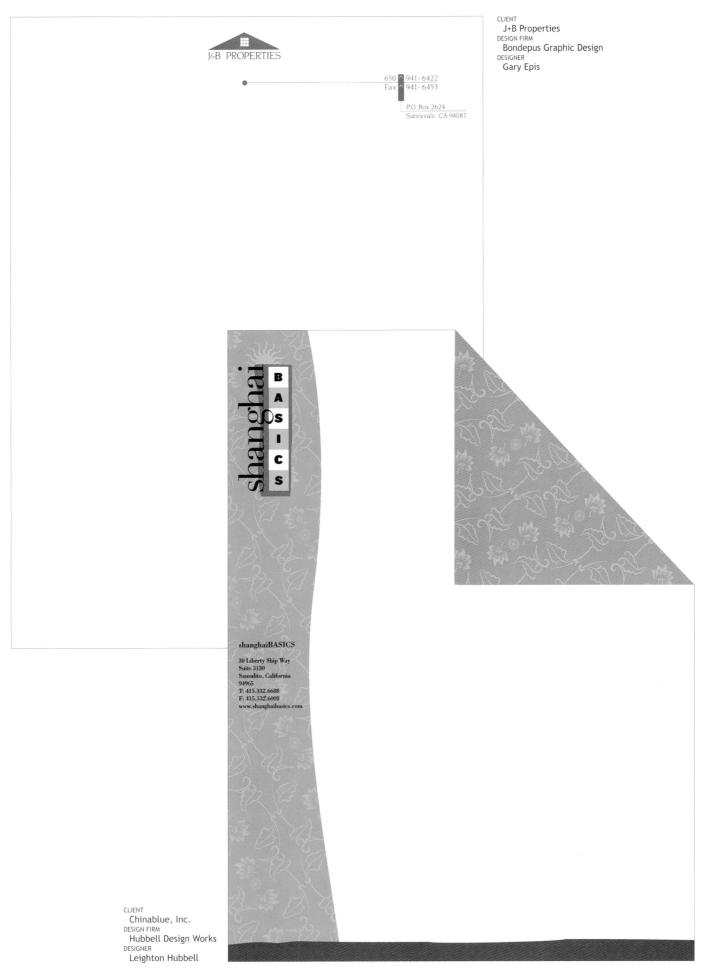

J&B PROPERTIES

650 941- 6422
Fax 941- 6453

P.O. Box 2624
Sunnyvale, CA 94087

shanghaiBASICS

30 Liberty Ship Way
Suite 3130
Sausalito, California
94965
T: 415.332.6688
F: 415.332.6008
www.shanghaibasics.com

ascentives
corporate specialty solutions

CLIENT
Ascentives
DESIGN FIRM
Rule 29
DESIGNERS
Justin Ahrens, Jim Boboru,
Jon McGrath

702 N Midvale Blvd | Madison, WI 53705
T **608 231 2488** F 608 231 1382
ascentivescss.com

THE INN AT
RANCHO SANTA FE

P.O. Box 869
Rancho Santa Fe
California 92067
858-756-1131
fax 858-759-1604
www.theinnatrsf.com

CLIENT
Inn at Rancho Santa Fe
DESIGN FIRM
Hetz Advertising
DESIGNER
Michael Hetz

31405 18th Ave. So.

Federal Way, WA

98003-5433

Tel 253.945.2000

www.fwsd.wednet.edu

CLIENT
Federal Way Public Schools
DESIGN FIRM
Hansen Design Company
DESIGNERS
Pat Hansen, Jacqueline Smith

☐ **BEGGS MOTOR HOMES**
11197 Cleveland Ave. NW
Uniontown, OH 44685-0545
Phone 330-499-9755
Fax 330-499-6002
Toll Free 800-331-3168

☐ **BEGGS RV CENTER**
6075 Dressler Rd. NW
North Canton, OH 44720
Phone 330-494-3811
Fax 330-494-8255
Toll Free 800-837-8100

www.beggsmotorhomes.com

CLIENT
Beggs
DESIGN FIRM
Innis Maggiore Group
DESIGNERS
Jeff Monter,
Cheryl Molnar

Jennifer
NICHOLSON

CLIENT
Jennifer Nicholson
DESIGN FIRM
[i]e design, Los Angeles
DESIGNER
Marcie Carson

1311 B Montana Avenue
Santa Monica, CA 90403

Tel 310-576-7116

Fax 310-576-7126

> m e d i a f l o w

p > 2 1 6 . 4 6 4 . 5 2 9 6
f > 2 1 6 . 4 6 4 . 6 2 8 1

CLIENT
>mediaflow
DESIGN FIRM
Studio Graphique
DESIGNER
Gina Gerken

2 4 4 0 0 H i g h p o i n t R d © S u i t e 3 © B e a c h w o o d , O H 4 4 1 2 2 © m e d i a f l o w . n e t

CIRCLECINEMA

P.O. BOX 50750 | TULSA, OKLAHOMA 74150 | 918.592.FILM OR 918.592.3456

CLIENT
Circle Cinema
DESIGN FIRM
Walsh Associates, Inc.
DESIGNER
Kerry Walsh

THE LEYO GROUP

LeYo

2744 N. Lincoln Avenue • Suite 200 • Chicago
Phone: 773.477.7717 • Fax: 773.477.7751 • htt

CLIENT
The Leyo Group, Inc.
DESIGN FIRM
The Leyo Group, Inc.
DESIGNERS
Mike Kelly, Horst Mickler,
Bill Leyo

TIMOTHY PAUL
CARPETS + TEXTILES

1404 14th Street NW • Washington DC 20005
TEL 202.319.1100   FAX 202.319.1110
EMAIL info@timothypaulcarpets.com
www.timothypaulcarpets.com

CLIENT
Timothy Paul Carpets & Textiles
DESIGN FIRM
Design Nut
DESIGNER
Brent M. Almond

1700 Connecticut Avenue NW • Suite 300 • Washington DC • 20009

Washington DC • Tysons Corner Va

direct: 202.745.0130
fax: 202.745.0112

STRUCTURE
communications group, llc

structuredesign.com

CLIENT
Structure Communications Group, LLC
DESIGN FIRM
Structure Communications Group, LLC
DESIGNERS
Michael Chinn, Alex Peltekian

GECKO
creative

fax 410·796·9278

tel 410·796·4691

www.geckocreative.com

ellicott city, maryland 21043

7936 brightlight place,

CINCINNATI *Ballet*

1555 CENTRAL PARKWAY CINCINNATI, OHIO 45214·2863
P. 513·621·5219 F. 513·621·4844 W. CINCINNATIBALLET.COM
BOX OFFICE P. 513·621·5282 F. 513·621·6323

40th
1963 2003
ANNIVERSARY

VICTORIA MORGAN—ARTISTIC DIRECTOR
CARMON DELEONE—MUSIC DIRECTOR
ALAN R. HILLS—EXECUTIVE DIRECTOR

PEOPLE • PROCESS • PREMIER PERFORMANCE

CLIENT
  TAGA Consulting
DESIGN FIRM
  Matthew Huberty Design
DESIGNER
  Matthew Huberty

Star Tribune
425 Portland Avenue
Minneapolis, MN 55488-0002

INTERACTIVE & DIRECT MARKETING
startribune.com/interactive

StarTribune
MINNEAPOLIS • ST. PAUL

CLIENT
  Star Tribune Interactive
  & Direct Marketing Department
DESIGN FIRM
  Star Tribune Creative Group
DESIGNER
  Lisa Ruetlen

CLIENT
Bell Memorials & Granite Works
DESIGN FIRM
designfive
DESIGNER
Ron Nikkel

BELL MEMORIALS
& GRANITE WORKS

850 SAN JOSE AVE.
SUITE 110
CLOVIS, CA 93612
(559) 299-7055
(559) 299-7045 FAX
bellgranite@sbcglobal.net

phone 585-473-5127
cell 585-281-9228
christine@NotYourAverageTrinket.com

CLIENT
Not Your Average Trinket—
Christine Giangreco
DESIGN FIRM
Kraus/LeFevre Studios
DESIGNERS
Tracie Smith, Mark Coon

CLIENT
Sargent & Berman
DESIGN FIRM
Sargent & Berman
DESIGNERS
Peter Sargent,
Barbara Chan

Apian◈

Apian Software, Inc.
400 N. 34th St.
Suite 310
Seattle, WA 98103

TEL (206) 547-5321
TOLL-FREE (800) 237-4565
FAX (206) 547-8493
WEB www.apian.com

Sargent & Berman, Inc. > *design and marketing consultant*
1337 Third Street Promenade, Santa Monica, California
t 310 576 1070 *f* 310 576 1074
> www.sargentberman.com

CLIENT
Apian Software
DESIGN FIRM
Platform Creative Group
DESIGNER
Jin Kwon

a°dk

Wine Fest No. 8

A TOAST TO CHILDREN'S HEALTH

may thirty & thirty one

VINTAGE 2003

MINNEAPOLIS
CONVENTION
CENTER

University Pediatrics Foundation
MMC 727
420 Delaware Street SE
Minneapolis, MN 55455
tele: 612.624.6900
fax: 612.626.1144
www.thewinefest.com

WINE ADVISORY
COMMITTEE

David Anderson
France 44 Wine & Market
Alicia Anderson
France 44 Wine & Market
Tim Bevins
Tonka Bottle Shop
Mike Clausen
Phillips Wine & Spirits
Larry Colbeck
The Wine Company
Phil Colich
Hennepin-Lake Liquor
Coleman Craft
The Wine Company
Jerry DeRose
Griggs Cooper
Corinne Erhart
World Class Wines
Tim Fagely
Beringer Wine Estates
Steve Farver
Bellboy Corporation
Alfred Fish
UPF WineFest Advisor
Chris Griese
World Class Wines
Don Hartzel
Grand Pere Wines
Les Hill
Wine Merchants
John Hoffman
Winery Associates
Daniel Horsch
Quality Wine & Spirits
Kathy Huber
Liquor Depot
Steve Johnson
Liquor Depot
Andrew Kass
Sutler's Wines & Spirits
Lee Kitzenberg
Community Volunteer
Joe Kotnik
World Wide Cellars
Dan Manning
Haskell's
Tom McFadden
*Johnson Brothers
Liquor Company*
John Mills
MGM Liquor Warehouse
Robert Nicols
*Chateau Julien
Wine Estates*
Bill Paustis
Paustis Wine Company
Bob Plantenberg
*Robert Mondavi
Family of Wines*
Dale Roberts
Community Volunteer
Bob Staples
Phillips Wine & Spirits
Mike Thomas
Thomas Liquors
Marty Ullman
World Class Wines
Brad Weiss
WineStreet Spirits
Steve Wilbon
Wine Merchants

CLIENT
Platform Creative Group
DESIGN FIRM
Platform Creative Group
DESIGNERS
Jin Kwon, Todd Karam,
Robert Dietz, Kathy Thompson

Platform Creative Group, Inc.
80 South Jackson Suite 308
Seattle, Washington 98104

206.621.1855 (on you)
866.621.1855 (on us)
206.621.7146 (on paper)

CITY OF JEFFERSONVILLE

PARKS AND RECREATION

Rick Elliott
Superintendent

Thomas R. Galligan
Mayor

812 - 285 - 6440 office
812 - 285 - 6481 fax
www.jeffparks.org

1406 Frederick Avenue
Jeffersonville, Indiana 47130

An equal opportunity employer.

CLIENT
Dept. of Parks & Recreation—
City of Jeffersonville, Indiana
DESIGN FIRM
Smith Design Associates
DESIGNER
Cheryl Smith

CLIENT
Barbagelata Construction
DESIGN FIRM
Bondepus Graphic Design
DESIGNER
Gary Epis

Barbagelata
CONSTRUCTION

2618 McAlister St
San Francisco
California 94118

P 415.668.6115
F 415.668.6602

License no. 745230

MacDonald
PHOTOGRAPHY

22W540 POSS STREET
GLEN ELLYN, IL 60137

P 630-790-9519
F 630-790-2188
www.macpix.com

CLIENT
MacDonald Photography
DESIGN FIRM
Rule 29
DESIGNERS
Justin Ahrens, Jim Boborci,
Jon McGrath, Andrea Boren

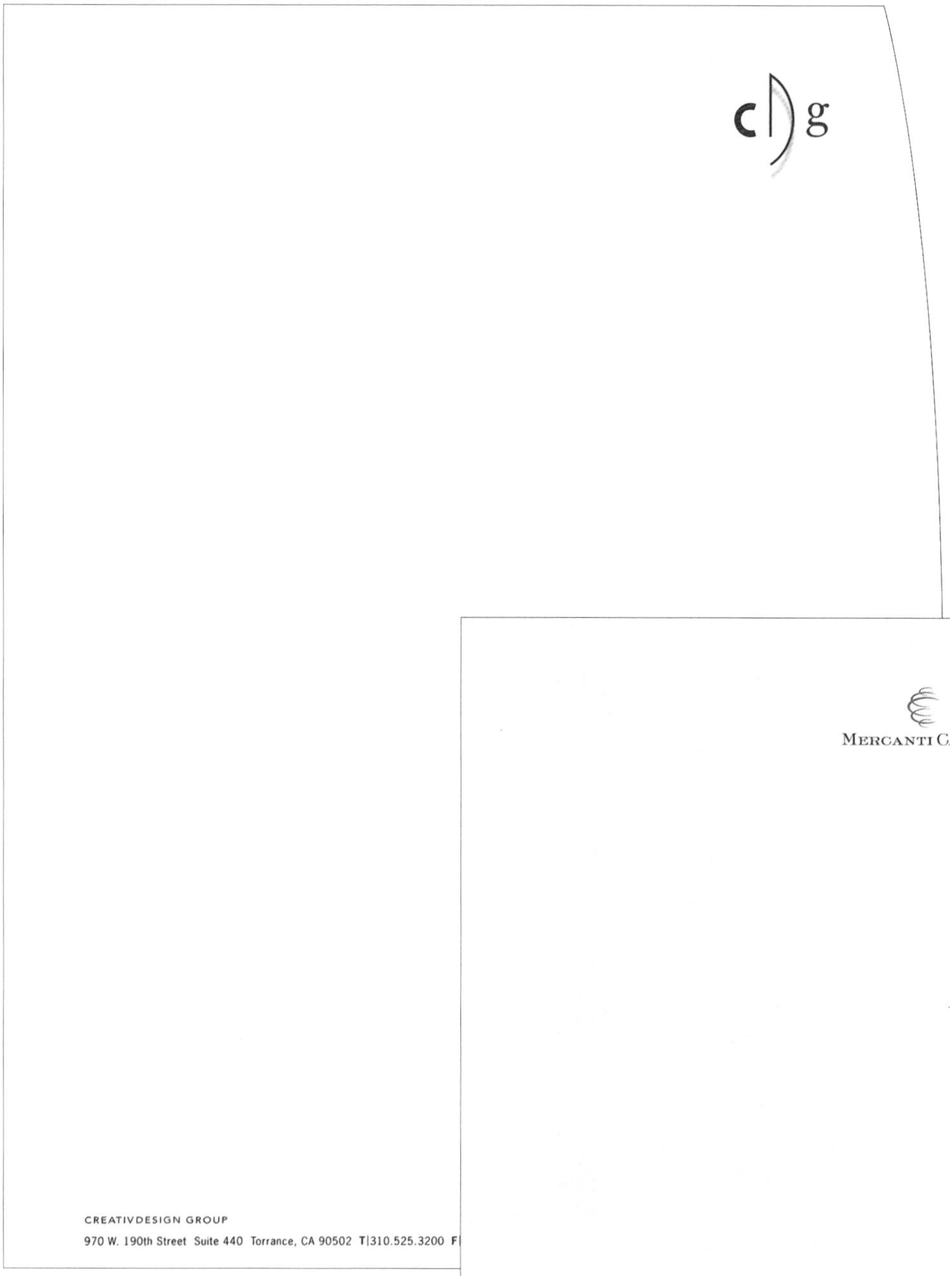

c⌐g

CLIENT
Creative Design Group
DESIGN FIRM
[i]e design, Los Angeles
DESIGNER
Richard Haynie

MERCANTI CAPITAL

CREATIVDESIGN GROUP
970 W. 190th Street Suite 440 Torrance, CA 90502 T|310.525.3200 F

CLIENT
Mercanti Capital
DESIGN FIRM
[i]e design, Los Angeles
DESIGNER
Cya Nelson

205   MINNEAPOLIS, MN 55403-1610   TEL: 612 333-0130   FAX: 612 333-0122

3115 NORTH WILKE ROAD, SUITE 5   P **847 577 7491**
ARLINGTON HEIGHTS, IL 60004   F 847 577 7492

CLIENT
  Mindware Creative
DESIGN FIRM
  Rule 29
DESIGNERS
  Justin Ahrens, Jim Boborci,
  Jon McGrath

7201 W. FORT STREET
DETROIT, MICHIGAN 48209

313.841.7780 PHONE
313.841.7858 SALES FAX
313.841.2920 ACCOUNTING FAX
WWW.ROCKYPRODUCE.COM

7201 W. FORT STREET
DETROIT, MICHIGAN 48209

CLIENT
  Rocky Produce
DESIGN FIRM
  Premier Communications Group
DESIGNERS
  Randy Fossano, Patrick Hatfield

CLIENT
IMIH Group
DESIGN FIRM
Premier Communications Group
DESIGNER
Joe Becker

iMiH
GROUP

29214 Lyon Oaks Drive
Wixom, Michigan 48393

phone: 248.437.2200
fax: 248.437.2299

www.imihgroup.com

Navigating Business Technology™

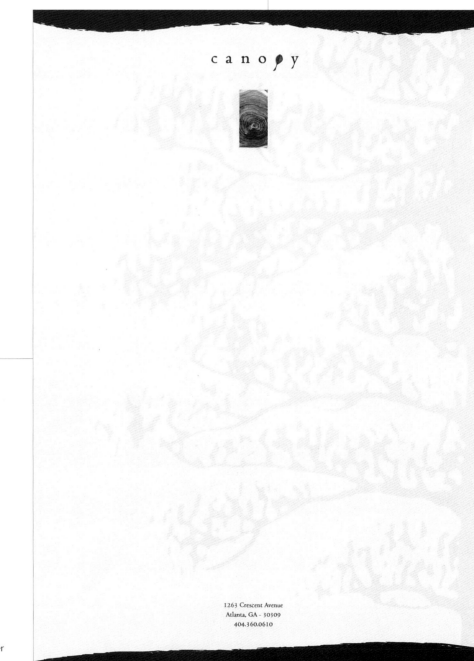

canopy

1263 Crescent Avenue
Atlanta, GA - 30309
404.360.0610

DESIGN FIRM
Portfolio Center
DESIGNER
Marshall Wolfe

KNOWLEDGE
CREATIVITY
TECHNOLOGY

123 North Washington Street
Boston, MA 02114-2113
617-646-4000 fax: 617-646-4040
www.artplustechnology.com

CLIENT
Art Plus Technology, Inc.
DESIGN FIRM
Art Plus Technology, Inc.
DESIGNER
Robert H. Linsky

11800 Wills Road | Suite 150 | Alpharetta, GA 30004 | 404-943-0225 | 404-943-1774 fax | 1-866-IC CHIPS www.falconsolutions.com

CLIENT
Falcon Solutions
DESIGN FIRM
Design Coup
DESIGNERS
Michael Higgins,
Patrick Foster

All in Good Taste
PRODUCTIONS

CLIENT
All in Good Taste Productions
DESIGN FIRM
Kolano Design
DESIGNER
Adrienne Ciuprinskas

 **teamfuel** 301 Main Street, Suite 212 | Huntington Beach, CA 92648 | 800-576-3835 | Fax 714-960-4271

1517 Monterey Street, Pitts
1145 San Jacinto Way, Palm

CLIENT
Team Fuel
DESIGN FIRM
Design Coup
DESIGNERS
Michael Higgins,
Patrick Foster

YOUR FUEL CHAMPION

Out of the Box

Package Design
Brand Identity

215 Hanford Drive
Fairfield, CT 06824
P: 203.254.1437
F: 203.256.8055
Email: info@ootbdesign.com
www.ootbdesign.com

CLIENT
Out Of The Box
DESIGN FIRM
Out Of The Box
DESIGNER
Rick Schneider

SQA | with you every step of the way

www.sqassociates.com

Software Quality Associates

125 Whipple Street   t   888.299.7638
Providence, RI 02908   f   401.273.4075

CLIENT
SQA
DESIGN FIRM
Im-aj Communications
& Design, Inc.
DESIGNERS
Jami Ouellette,
Mark Bevington

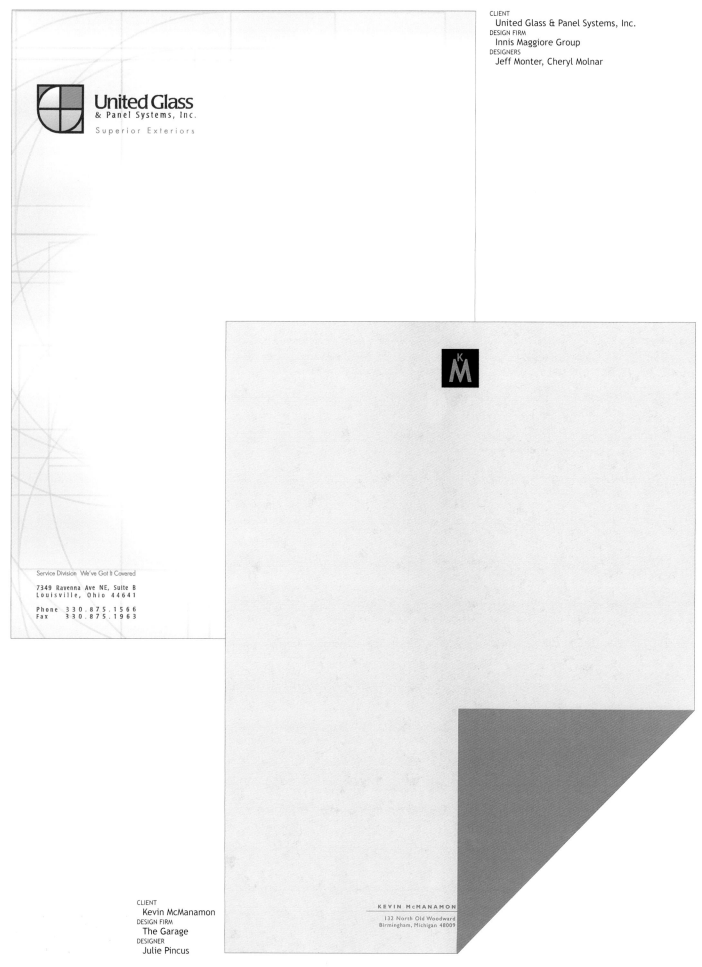

CLIENT
United Glass & Panel Systems, Inc.
DESIGN FIRM
Innis Maggiore Group
DESIGNERS
Jeff Monter, Cheryl Molnar

United Glass
& Panel Systems, Inc.
Superior Exteriors

Service Division We've Got It Covered

7349 Ravenna Ave NE, Suite B
Louisville, Ohio 44641

Phone 330.875.1566
Fax 330.875.1963

CLIENT
Kevin McManamon
DESIGN FIRM
The Garage
DESIGNER
Julie Pincus

KEVIN McMANAMON
132 North Old Woodward
Birmingham, Michigan 48009

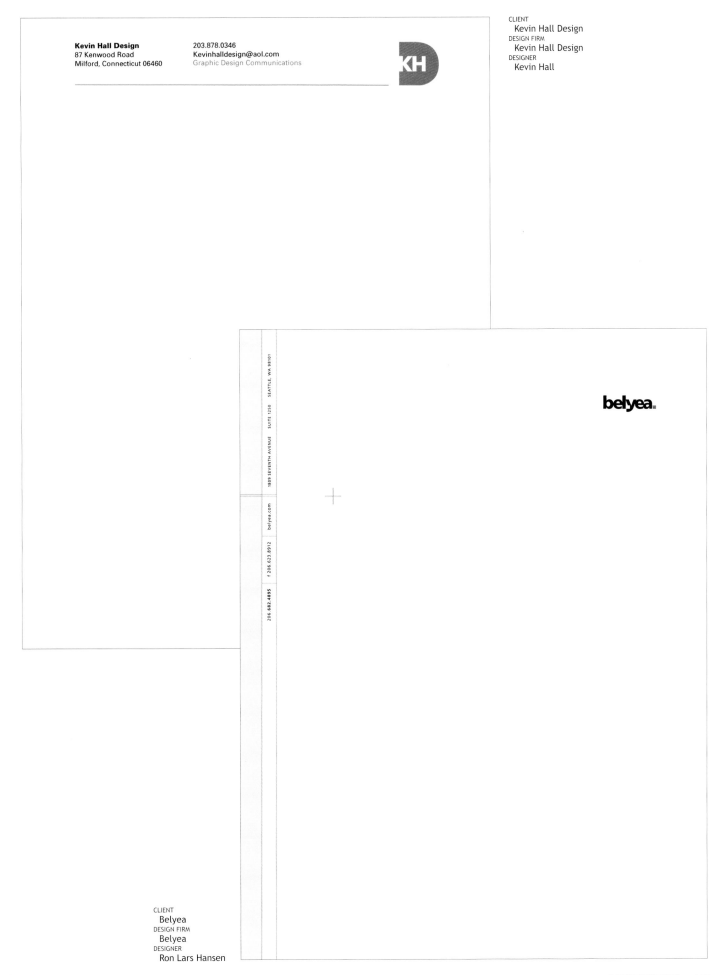

Kevin Hall Design
87 Kenwood Road
Milford, Connecticut 06460

203.878.0346
Kevinhalldesign@aol.com
Graphic Design Communications

KH

CLIENT
  Kevin Hall Design
DESIGN FIRM
  Kevin Hall Design
DESIGNER
  Kevin Hall

belyea.

1809 SEVENTH AVENUE   SUITE 1250   SEATTLE, WA 98101

belyea.com

f 206.623.8912

206.682.4895

CLIENT
  Belyea
DESIGN FIRM
  Belyea
DESIGNER
  Ron Lars Hansen

CLIENT
Bondepus Graphic Design
DESIGN FIRM
Bondepus Graphic Design
DESIGNERS
Gary Epis, Amy Bond

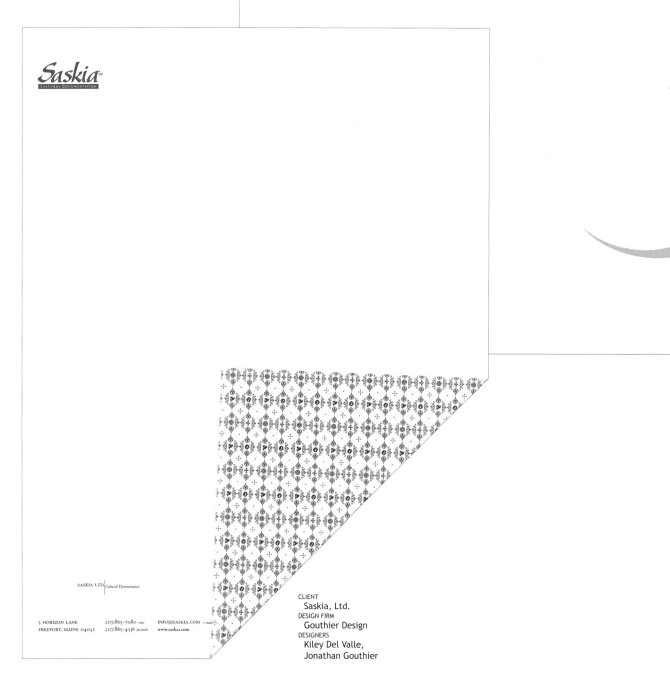

807 Haight Street, Suite II
San Francisco, CA 94117
415.864.5539*P

CLIENT
Saskia, Ltd.
DESIGN FIRM
Gouthier Design
DESIGNERS
Kiley Del Valle,
Jonathan Gouthier

SASKIA LTD | Cultural Documentation

5 HORIZON LANE   207.865-7080 voice   INFO@SASKIA.COM   e-mail
FREEPORT, MAINE 04032 207.865-4356 facsimile www.saskia.com

CLIENT
Da Vinci Gourmet, Ltd.
DESIGN FIRM
Da Vinci Creative
DESIGNERS
Jack Oelschlager,
Jennifer Harowicz

Da Vinci Gourmet, Ltd.
7224 First Avenue South, Seattle, Washington 98108 - (206) 768-7401 - (800) 640-6779 - Fax (206) 764-3989 - www.davincigourmet.com

ins◊urce

defining the future of written communications

SOLUTIONS

ood Avenue
21224
30   f 410 342 6341   1 877 610 5974

info@insourcesolutions.com
www.insourcesolutions.com

CLIENT
inSource solutions
DESIGN FIRM
re: salzman designs
DESIGNERS
Ida Cheinman,
Rick Salzman

CLIENT
Chen Design Associates
DESIGN FIRM
Chen Design Associates
DESIGNERS
Leon Yu, Josh Chen

589 HOWARD STREET FOURTH FLOOR | SAN FRANCISCO CALIFORNIA 94105-3001

CHEN DESIGN ASSOCIATES

1140 CASTRO ST. // SAN FRANCISCO // CALIFORNIA // 94114 // USA // WWW.PENABRAND.COM // TEL.415.206.1632 // COMM SYSTEM // NO. 0786-02

CLIENT
Peñabrand
DESIGN FIRM
Peñabrand/Butler, Shine & Stern
DESIGNER
Luis Peña

The Reynolds Group Inc

CLIENT
The Reynolds Group
DESIGN FIRM
Jones Design Group
DESIGNERS
Katherin Staggs,
Vicky Jones

CATHERINE BOWEN
THE PROUD PROCURER OF
WORDS
AND OTHER IMPORTANT THINGS

4185 FAIRWAY VILLAS DR. ALPHARETTA. GA 30022
V 770.750.0184 f 770.750.0185

CLIENT
Catherine Bowen
DESIGN FIRM
Peñabrand/Butler, Shine & Stern
DESIGNER
Luis Peña

catherinembowen@hotmail.com TEL 415.383.1667   95 SUNNYSIDE AVE. MILL VALLEY, CALIFORNIA 94941

International Spy Museum

INTERNATIONAL
SPY
MUSEUM

Graphic Response

@jgstanley.com   P] 212.679.0079
um.org   F] 212.679.0296

||| 4460 Commerce Circle
★ Atlanta ★ Georgia 30336
www.graphicresponse.com

404 phone
696.9000
696.4924
fax

5849 Smithway Street
Los Angeles CA 90040-1605
Tel 323.727.0007 Fax 323.727.0011

billy blues

MDC Wallcoverings

MDC Wallcoverings

1200 Arthur Avenue
Elk Grove, Illinois 60007
tel 847.437.4000
fax 847.437.4017

www.mdcwall.com

1744 South Sherman Denver Colorado 80210 phone 303-715-4472 fax 720-294-0154

CLIENT
B Hawkins Inc.
DESIGN FIRM
Asher Studio
DESIGNER
Gretchen Wills

b hawkins inc

FIRST AMERICAN FUNDS™

P.O. Box 3011
Milwaukee, Wisconsin 53201-3011

800.677.FUND

www.firstamericanfunds.com

CLIENT
U.S. Bancorp Asset Management
DESIGN FIRM
Larsen Design + Interactive
DESIGNERS
Jo Davison, Todd Nesser

CORPORATE IDENTITY
MANUALS

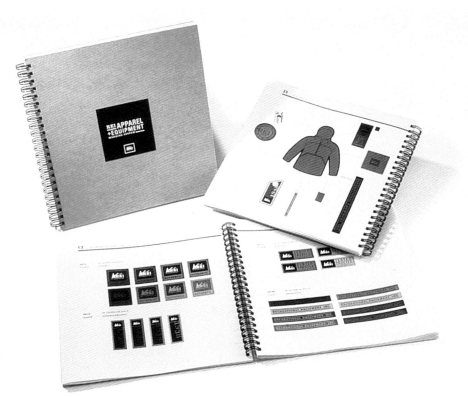

CLIENT
Recreational Equipment, Inc.
DESIGN FIRM
Lemley Design Company
DESIGNERS
David Lemley, Yuri Shvets,
Matthew Loyd, Tobi Brown,
Jenny Hill

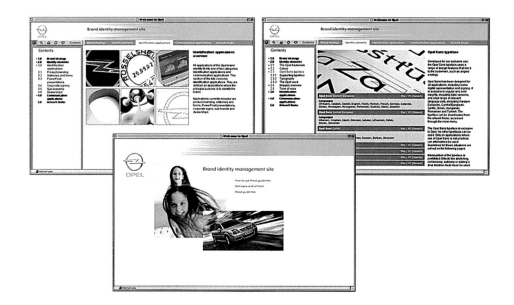

CLIENT
Adam Opel AG
DESIGN FIRM
FutureBrand Hypermedia
DESIGNERS
Carol Wolf, Tom Li,
Miles Perkins, Rupert Spurling,
Nunzio Miano

Member
**Children's Hospital
of NewYork-Presbyterian**

Stationery Guidelines

January 2002

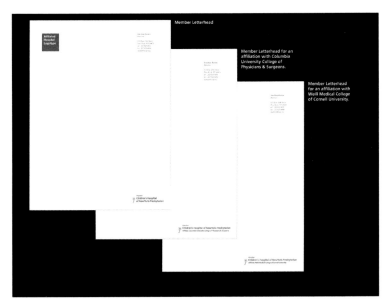

Member Letterhead

Member Letterhead for an
affiliation with Columbia
University College of
Physicians & Surgeons.

Member Letterhead
for an affiliation with
Weill Medical College
of Cornell University.

MICHAEL JOHNSON, MD
Medical Director

**Affiliated
Medical Center**

One Medical Center Drive
Centertown, New York 12345
tel: 607 123 4567
fax: 607 891 0111
email: dr_michael_johnson@affimedcenter.org

Member
Children's Hospital
of NewYork-Presbyterian

AFFILIATED HEALTH SYSTEM   Health System Logotype

Affiliated Hospital
One Medical Center Drive
P.O.Box 9876
Centertown, New York 12345
212/821-0651
dr_michael_johnson@afilmedcenter.org

Michael S. Johnson, MD, FAAP
Chairman, Department of Pediatrics

Member
Children's Hospital of NewYork-Presbyterian
Affiliate: Weill Medical College of Cornell University

AFFILIATED HOSPITAL ASSOCIATES

One Medical Center Drive
P.O.Box 9876
Center Town, New York 12345
tel 607 123 4567
fax 607 891 0111

Michael S. Johnson, MD, FAAP

Member
Children's Hospital of NewYork-Presbyterian
Affiliate: Columbia University College of Physicians & Surgeons

Sample Business Cards

CLIENT
Children's Hospital of
New York—Presbyterian
DESIGN FIRM
Arnold Saks Associates
DESIGNER
Molly Wakeman

CLIENT
Coca-Cola
DESIGN FIRM
FutureBrand
DESIGNERS
Michael Thibodean,
Marie Schabenbeck

CLIENT
T. Rowe Price
DESIGN FIRM
Grafik
DESIGNERS
Michele Mar, Alysia Orrel,
Lynn Umemoto, Judy Kirpich

CLIENT
FedExForum
DESIGN FIRM
Landor Associates
DESIGNERS
Rafael Baeza, Graham Atkinson,
Rachel Wear, Margaret Youngblood,
Tom Venegas, Caroline Yarker

CLIENT
 Recreational Equipment, Inc.
DESIGN FIRM
 Lemley Design Company
DESIGNERS
 David Lemley, Yuri Shvets,
 Matthew Loyd, Tobi Brown,
 Jenny Hill

CLIENT
 Mexican Tourism Board
DESIGN FIRM
 FutureBrand Hypermedia
DESIGNERS
 Carol Wolf, Tom Li,
 Steve Aaron

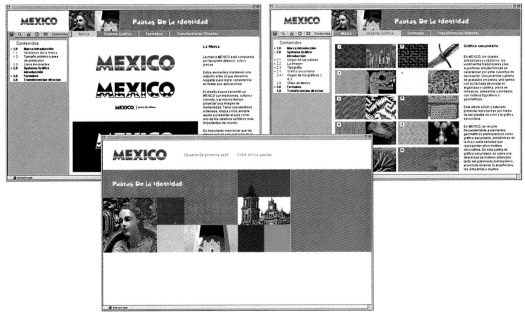

CLIENT
Manulife Financial
DESIGN FIRM
RainCastle Communications
DESIGNER
Rotem Meller

CLIENT
James Madison University
DESIGN FIRM
JMU Division of University Advancement
DESIGNER
Carolyn Windmiller

CLIENT
Mattel
DESIGN FIRM
Hamagami/Carroll
DESIGNERS
Christine Kim, Carly Devery,
Barbara Odza

CLIENT
New York–Presbyterian
DESIGN FIRM
Arnold Saks Associates
DESIGNER
Molly Wakeman

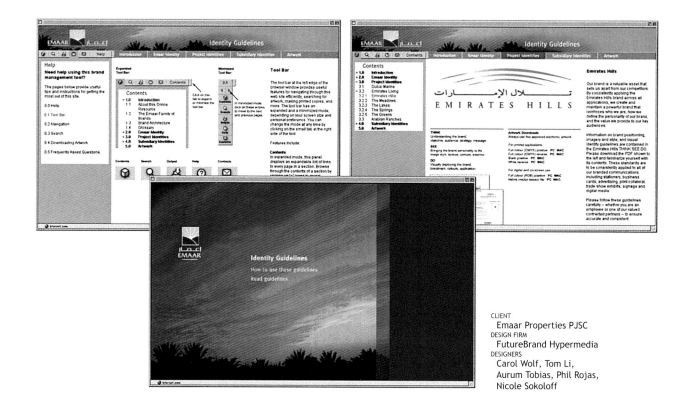

CLIENT
  Emaar Properties PJSC
DESIGN FIRM
  FutureBrand Hypermedia
DESIGNERS
  Carol Wolf, Tom Li,
  Aurum Tobias, Phil Rojas,
  Nicole Sokoloff

CLIENT
  Lion's Choice/Red Lion Beef Corp.
DESIGN FIRM
  Kiku Obata + Company
DESIGNERS
  Troy Guzman,
  Joe Floresca

CLIENT
Aultman Hospital
DESIGN FIRM
Innis Maggiore Group
DESIGNER
Cheryl Molnar

CLIENT
Masland Carpets, Inc.
DESIGN FIRM
Perkins & Will/Eva Maddox
Branded Environments
DESIGNERS
Eileen Jones, Brian Weatherford,
Emily Neville, Malaika Corsentino

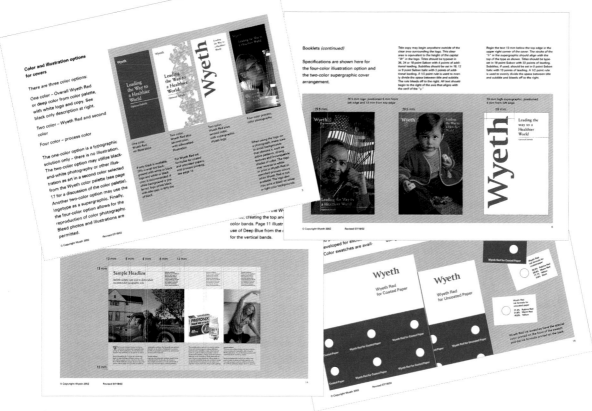

CLIENT
Wyeth
DESIGN FIRM
Arnold Saks Associates
DESIGNER
Robert Yasharian

CLIENT
Eastman Kodak Company
DESIGN FIRM
Forward branding & identity

CLIENT
CPP, Inc.
DESIGN FIRM
Mortensen Design, Inc.
DESIGNER
Helena Seo

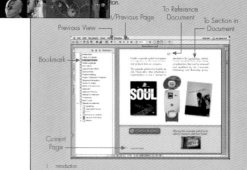

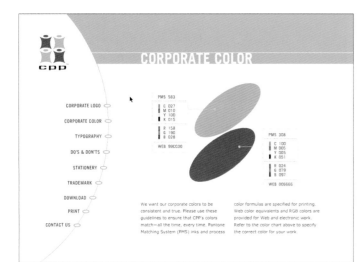

SIGNAGE & ENVIRONMENTAL GRAPHICS

CLIENT
Glimcher
DESIGN FIRM
Lorenc+Yoo Design
DESIGNERS
Jan Lorenc, Chung Yoo, David Park,
Sakchai Rangsiyakorn, Susie Norris,
Ken Boyd, Steve McCall, Gary Flesher

CLIENT
Aura
DESIGN FIRM
kor group
DESIGNERS
Jim Gibson, MB Jarosik,
Karen Dendy

CLIENT
Haworth
DESIGN FIRM
Lorenc+Yoo Design
DESIGNERS
Jan Lorenc, Chung Yoo, David Park,
Mark Malaer, Sakchai Rangsiyakorn,
Susie Norris, Ken Boyd, Steve McCall

CLIENT
Nestlé USA, Inc.—Beverage Division
DESIGN FIRM
Thompson Design Group
DESIGNERS
Dennis Thompson,
Trevor Thompson,
Gene DuPont

CLIENT
Regent Street Market
DESIGN FIRM
Welch Design Group
DESIGNER
Lisa Heitke

CLIENT
Team Lexus
DESIGN FIRM
Planit
DESIGNER
Molly Stevenson

CLIENT
University of Utah
DESIGN FIRM
Nassar Design
DESIGNERS
Nelida Nassar,
Margarita Enconienda

CLIENT
Round House Theatre
DESIGN FIRM
Kircher, Inc.
DESIGNER
Bruce E. Morgan

CLIENT
United Way
DESIGN FIRM
Rottman Creative Group, LLC
DESIGNER
Gary Rottman

CLIENT
LimeAide Refreshing Delivery
DESIGN FIRM
Performance Graphics
of Lake Norman, NC
DESIGNERS
Mitzi Mayhew,
Alec McAlister

CLIENT
Recreational Equipment, Inc.
DESIGN FIRM
Lemley Design Company
DESIGNERS
David Lemley, Yuri Shvets,
Matthew Loyd, Tobi Brown,
Jenny Hill

CLIENT
Applied Materials
DESIGN FIRM
Gee + Chung Design
DESIGNERS
Earl Gee,
Fani Chung

CLIENT
Sony Ericsson
DESIGN FIRM
Lorenc+Yoo Design
DESIGNERS
Jan Lorenc, Chung Yoo, David Park,
Mark Malaer, Sakchai Rangsiyakorn,
Susie Norris, Ken Boyd, Steve McCall

CLIENT
Meyer Bros. Dairy
DESIGN FIRM
Hillis Design
DESIGNERS
Anna Clark, John Hillis

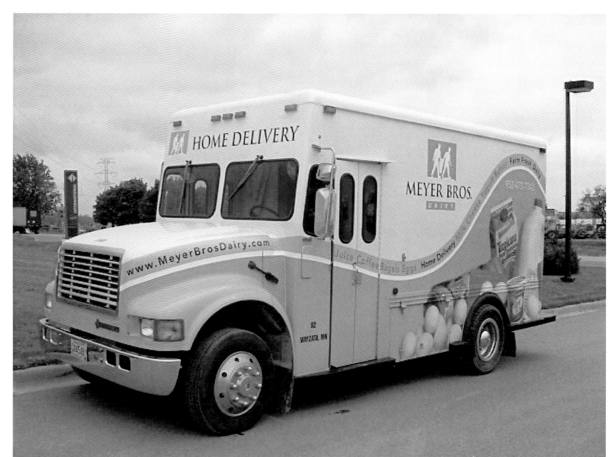

CLIENT
Wings Bar + Grille
DESIGN FIRM
Funk/Levis & Associates
DESIGNER
Christopher Berner

CLIENT
Recreational Equipment, Inc.
DESIGN FIRM
Lemley Design Company
DESIGNERS
David Lemley, Yuri Shvets,
Matthew Loyd, Tobi Brown,
Jenny Hill

CLIENT
City of Jeffersonville, Indiana
DESIGN FIRM
Smith Design Associates
DESIGNER
Cheryl Smith

CLIENT
Haworth
DESIGN FIRM
Lorenc+Yoo Design
DESIGNERS
Jan Lorenc, Chung Yoo, David Park,
Mark Malaer, Sakchai Rangsiyakorn,
Susie Norris, Ken Boyd, Steve McCall

CLIENT
Café Yumm!
DESIGN FIRM
Funk/Levis & Associates
DESIGNER
Christopher Berner

CLIENT
Cherry Creek Shopping Center
DESIGN FIRM
Ellen Bruss Design Team
DESIGNERS
Ellen Bruss,
Chris Guenther

CLIENT
Spoon—Restaurant
DESIGN FIRM
Bruce Yelaska Design
DESIGNER
Bruce Yelaska

CLIENT
Air Force Museum Foundation
DESIGN FIRM
VMA, Inc.
DESIGNERS
Rob Anspach, Kenneth Bolts,
Joel Warneke

CLIENT
City of Powder Springs
DESIGN FIRM
Jones Worley Design Inc.
DESIGNERS
Nelson Hagood,
Barry Worley

CLIENT
Green Bay Packers
DESIGN FIRM
ZD Studios, Inc.
DESIGNERS
Mark Schmitz,
Tina Remy

CLIENT
Trizechahn Development Corporation
DESIGN FIRM
ID8 Studio/RTKL
DESIGNERS
Paul F. Jacob III, Katherine J. Spraque,
Kevin Horn, Marla Nadolney, Mark Demarta,
Rodel Manalang, Xavier Garaud, Anthony Hsu

CLIENT
Marshall Field's
DESIGN FIRM
Shea, Inc.
DESIGNERS
Shawn King, Holly Robbins,
Mark Whitenack

CLIENT
Jacksonville Port Authority
DESIGN FIRM
Jones Worley Design Inc.
DESIGNERS
Chris Bowles,
Barry Worley

CLIENT
Palisades Realty
DESIGN FIRM
Kiku Obata + Company
DESIGNERS
Kiku Obata, Todd Mayberry,
Rich Nelson, Troy Guzman,
Amber Elli, Denise Fuehne,
Carole Jerome

CLIENT
Procter & Gamble
DESIGN FIRM
Interbrand Hulefeld
DESIGNER
Fedy Singson

CLIENT
FedExForum
DESIGN FIRM
Landor Associates
DESIGNERS
Rafael Baeza, Graham Atkinson,
Rachel Wear, Margaret Youngblood,
Tom Venegas, Caroline Yarker

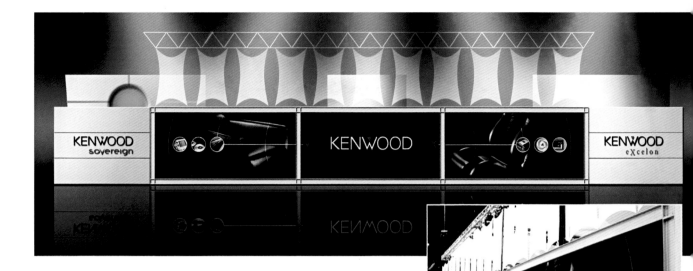

CLIENT
Kenwood USA
DESIGN FIRM
Jensen Design Associates, Inc.
DESIGNERS
Joel Penos, Dave Jensen

CLIENT
Irvine Company
DESIGN FIRM
ID8 Studio/RTKL
DESIGNERS
Paul F. Jacob III, Katherine J. Sprague,
Kevin Horn, Dave Schmitz

CLIENT
Bush Industries, Inc.
DESIGN FIRM
Perkins & Will/Eva Maddox
Branded Environments
DESIGNERS
Eileen Jones, Brian Weatherford,
Carly Cannell, Anna Kania

CLIENT
Smithsonian National Zoo
DESIGN FIRM
JillTanenbaum Graphic Design + Adv.
DESIGNERS
Jill Tanenbaum,
Sue Sprinkle

Watching Elephants

CLIENT
  Green Bay Packers
DESIGN FIRM
  ZD Studios, Inc.
DESIGNERS
  Mark Schmitz,
  Tina Remy

CLIENT
  Eastman Kodak Company
DESIGN FIRM
  Forward branding & identity

CLIENT
  Reuters North America
  and Instinet Corp.
DESIGN FIRM
  ESI Design

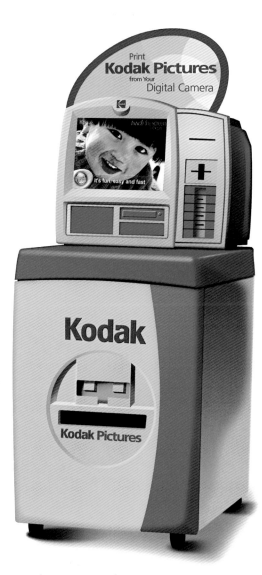

CLIENT
Diplomat Properties Ltd.
DESIGN FIRM
Lebowitz/Gould/Design, Inc.
DESIGNERS
Sue Gould,
Susan May

CLIENT
Safeco Insurance Company
DESIGN FIRM
Mayer/Reed
DESIGNERS
Michael Reed,
Debbie Fox Shaw

CLIENT
Target
DESIGN FIRM
Graphiculture
DESIGNERS
Sharon McKendry,
Cheryl Watson

CORPORATE IMAGE
BROCHURES

The power of McKesson.   Everywhere in healthcare.

CLIENT
McKesson
DESIGN FIRM
Cahan & Associates
DESIGNERS
Sharrie Brooks,
Bill Cahan

CLIENT
in3 corp.
DESIGN FIRM
gripdesign
DESIGNER
Kelly Kaminski

CLIENT
Emerson College
DESIGN FIRM
kor group
DESIGNERS
MB Jarosik, James Grady

CLIENT
Tree Top
DESIGN FIRM
Hornall Anderson
Design Works, Inc.
DESIGNERS
Katha Dalton,
Jana Nishi,
Michael Brugman

Wisely LETTER FROM THE CEO

Tree Top was able to generate profits again this year, despite a short crop and a tough economic environment. Bringing dollars to the bottom line isn't getting any easier. Competition is global and unremitting. Distribution channels have consolidated. Consumers are more fickle. So my hat's off to your Board of Directors, the people of Tree Top, and the processes that we've initiated over the last several years. Together they made it possible for us to add sufficient value to your fruit — efficiently enough — to generate profits. We will once again pay out these profits in cash to Cooperative members.

THE RESEARCH PARTNERSHIP PROGRAM

Closing in
on a Cure

we have
mind is
victory.

CLIENT
Juvenile Diabetes Research
Foundation International
DESIGN FIRM
Levine & Associates
DESIGNERS
Kari Riegler

X DESIGN COMPANY

strategy | positioning | identity | creative | communications

CLIENT
X Design Company
DESIGN FIRM
X Design Company
DESIGNER
Alex Valderrama

CLIENT
KidsPeace
DESIGN FIRM
Workhorse Design
DESIGNERS
Constance Kovar,
Anthony Taibi

CLIENT
Bob Kolbrener Photography
DESIGN FIRM
Berkeley Design LLC
DESIGNER
Larry Torno

CLIENT
Emaar Properties PJSC
DESIGN FIRM
FutureBrand Hypermedia
DESIGNERS
Nicole Sokoloff, Aurom Tobias,
Carlson Yu, Alicia Chang,
Dave Cox

CLIENT
Pittsburgh Downtown Partnership
DESIGN FIRM
Elias/Savion Advertising
DESIGNER
Ronnie Savion

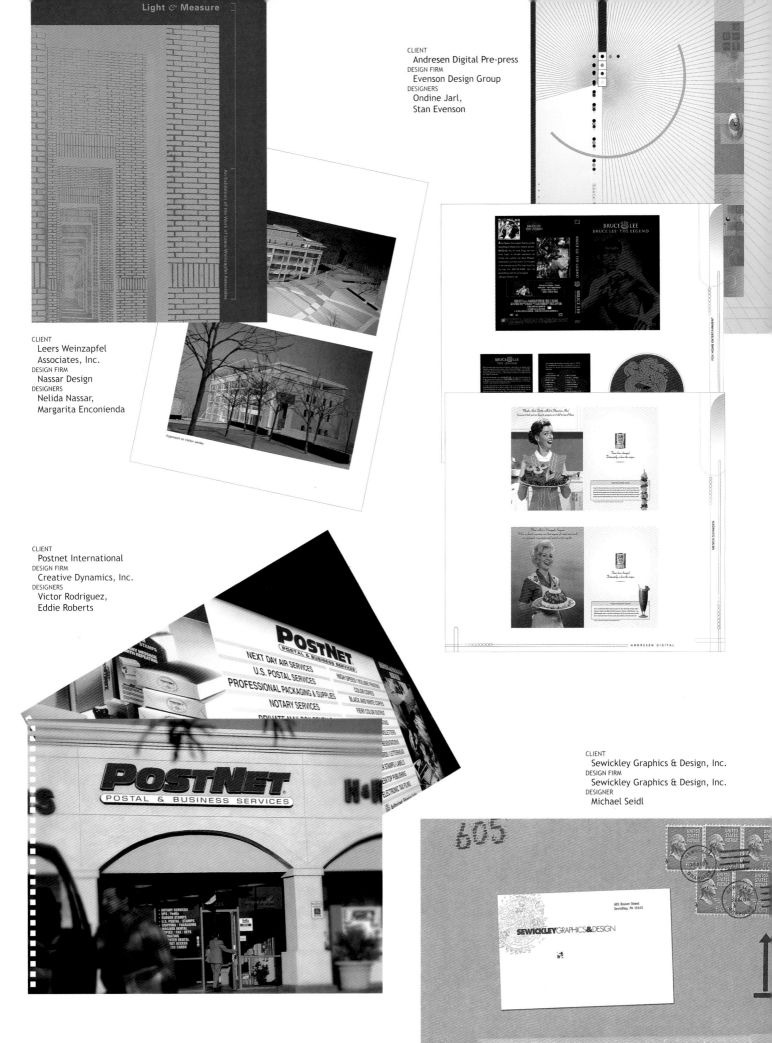

CLIENT
Andresen Digital Pre-press
DESIGN FIRM
Evenson Design Group
DESIGNERS
Ondine Jarl,
Stan Evenson

CLIENT
Leers Weinzapfel
Associates, Inc.
DESIGN FIRM
Nassar Design
DESIGNERS
Nelida Nassar,
Margarita Enconienda

CLIENT
Postnet International
DESIGN FIRM
Creative Dynamics, Inc.
DESIGNERS
Victor Rodriguez,
Eddie Roberts

CLIENT
Sewickley Graphics & Design, Inc.
DESIGN FIRM
Sewickley Graphics & Design, Inc.
DESIGNER
Michael Seidl

CLIENT
U-Save Auto Rental
DESIGN FIRM
Empire Communications Group
DESIGNERS
Phil Helow,
Elvin Letchford

bring art to life
FOR EVERYONE

CLIENT
The Minneapolis Institute of Arts
DESIGN FIRM
Larsen Design + Interactive
DESIGNERS
Liina Koukkari, Todd Mannes,
Ann Bauleke

CLIENT
Seattle Sonics
DESIGN FIRM
Hornall Anderson Design Works, Inc.
DESIGNERS
Jack Anderson, Mark Popich,
Andrew Wicklund, Don Kenoyer

CLIENT
Piper Rudnick LLP
DESIGN FIRM
Greenfield/Belser Ltd
DESIGNERS
Burkey Belser,
John Bruns

CLIENT
The Society of Typographic Arts
DESIGN FIRM
dawndesign
DESIGNERS
Dawn Peccatiello,
Cheri Gearhart

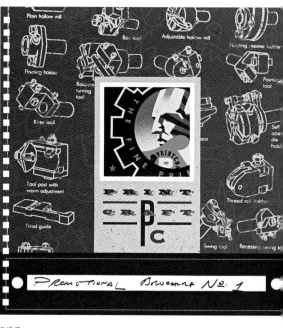

CLIENT
Print Craft
DESIGN FIRM
Brad Norr Design
DESIGNERS
Brad D. Norr, Andrew Bessler,
Dan Anderson

CLIENT
Rockford Symphony Orchestra
DESIGN FIRM
Conflux Design
DESIGNER
Greg Fedorev

CLIENT
Middlesex County Democratic Organi
DESIGN FIRM
Ted DeCagna Graphic Design
DESIGNERS
Ted DeCagna,
Dave Robertson

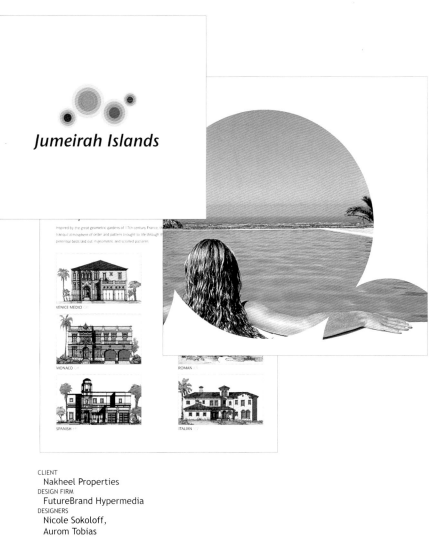

Jumeirah Islands

Inspired by the great geometric gardens of 17th century France, the tranquil atmosphere of order and pattern brought to life through the perennial beds laid out in geometric and scrolled patterns.

VENICE MEDICI

MONACO

ROMAN

SPANISH

ITALIAN

CLIENT
Nakheel Properties
DESIGN FIRM
FutureBrand Hypermedia
DESIGNERS
Nicole Sokoloff,
Aurom Tobias

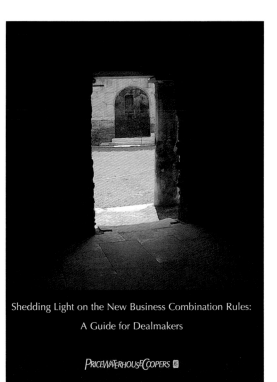

Shedding Light on the New Business Combination Rules:
A Guide for Dealmakers

PRICEWATERHOUSE COOPERS

CLIENT
CEO's & CFO's of Major Global Corp.
DESIGN FIRM
Pricewaterhouse Coopers
DESIGNER
Raquella Kagan

CLIENT
MOBITRAC Inc.
DESIGN FIRM
Avenue Group
DESIGNERS
Bob Domenz, Mike Gorgo,
Geoffrey Mark

LEVINE & ASSOCIATES, INC.   L&A   VISUAL COMMUNICATIONS

CLIENT
Levine & Associates
DESIGN FIRM
Levine & Associates
DESIGNERS
Monica Snellings, Lena Markley,
Dana Craig

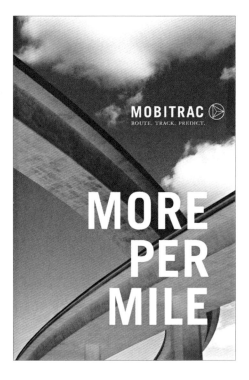

MOBITRAC
ROUTE. TRACK. PREDICT.

MORE
PER
MILE

BOULLIOUN

It's the lease we can do.

CLIENT
Boullioun Aviation Services
DESIGN FIRM
Hornall Anderson Design Works, Inc.
DESIGNERS
Jack Anderson, Katha Dalton,
Sonja Max, Hillary Radbill,
Henry Yiu, Michael Brugman

SONICS

HE DEFINITELY DOESN'T HAVE A FEAR OF

FLYING

SEASON TICKETS

IT'S LIKE YOU ARE HELPING GARY
DOUBLE TEAM
EXCEPT YOU'RE IN THE STANDS AND HE'S DOING MOST OF THE WORK

SONICS

CLIENT
Seattle Sonics
DESIGN FIRM
Hornall Anderson
Design Works, Inc.
DESIGNERS
Jack Anderson,
Mark Popich,
Andrew Wicklund

CLIENT
Linear Technology Corporation
DESIGN FIRM
Cahan & Associates
DESIGNERS
Todd Simmons, Bill Cahan

MCMANIS
FAMILY VINEYARDS

The confluence of two rivers, the San Joaquin and Stanislaus,
creates a unique microclimate that makes a most desirable area within
California's winegrowing regions. Four generations of the McManis
family have farmed this fertile land and made it their home.

CLIENT
McManis Family Vineyards
DESIGN FIRM
Marcia Herrmann Design
DESIGNER
Marcia Herrmann

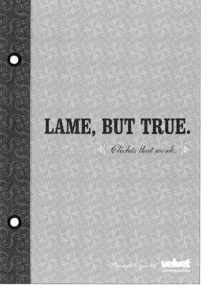

k outside the box

rite*fit
rite*fit
rite*fit
rite*fit
rite fit
rite fit
rite*fit
rite*fit
thousands of opportunities
rite*fit

hropycareers.com

hard-to-fill shoes

THE CHRONICLE OF PHILANTHROPY'S
philanthropycareers.com

LAME, BUT TRUE.
Clichés that work.

Brought to you by velvet

The Time Has Come

Lawrence Upper School

MOVE ME

CLIENT
Emaar Properties PJSC
DESIGN FIRM
FutureBrand Hypermedia
DESIGNERS
Nicole Sokoloff, Aurom Tobias,
Carson Yu, Alicia Chang, Dave Cox

CLIENT
Orivo
DESIGN FIRM
Hornall Anderson Design Works, Inc.
DESIGNERS
Jack Anderson, Andrew Wicklund,
Henry Yiu

CLIENT
Asher Studio
DESIGN FIRM
Asher Studio
DESIGNERS
Gretchen Wills,
Connie Asher

CLIENT
Gartner
DESIGN FIRM
Cahan & Associates
DESIGNERS
Bob Dinetz, Bill Cahan

CLIENT
Webster University
DESIGN FIRM
Paradowski Graphic Design
DESIGNER
Shawn Cornell

CLIENT
AMAC
DESIGN FIRM
Marcia Herrmann Design
DESIGNER
Marcia Herrmann

CLIENT
Lockheed Martin—
Naval Electronics & Surveillance Systems
DESIGN FIRM
Lockheed Martin
DESIGNER
Kevin Moore

CLIENT
Unitus
DESIGN FIRM
Belyea
DESIGNER
Ron Lars Hansen

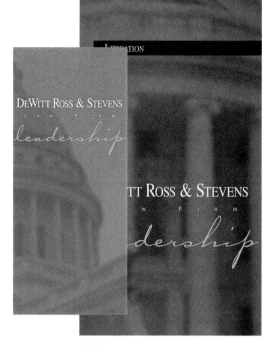

CLIENT
DeWitt Ross & Stevens
DESIGN FIRM
Welch Design Group
DESIGNER
Lisa Heitke

CLIENT
Spaelegance.com
DESIGN FIRM
Reinnov8
DESIGNER
Richard A. Hooper

CLIENT
K2 Corporation
DESIGN FIRM
Hornall Anderson Design Works, Inc.
DESIGNERS
**Jack Anderson, Andrew Smith,
Tiffany Scheiblauer, Andrew Wicklund,
Ed Lee**

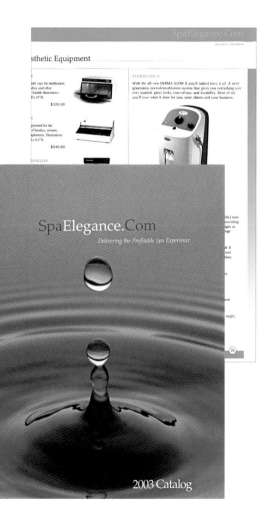

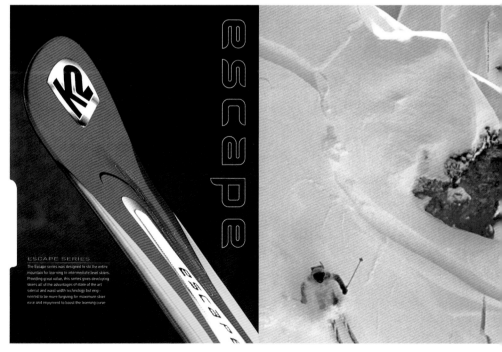

CLIENT
Nakheel Properties
DESIGN FIRM
FutureBrand Hypermedia
DESIGNER
Tom Li, Carlson Yu,
Alicia Chang, Brendan Ryan

CLIENT
Seattle Sonics
DESIGN FIRM
Hornall Anderson Design Works, Inc.
DESIGNERS
Jack Anderson, Mark Popich,
Andrew Wicklund, Don Kenoyer

CLIENT
Cyberxpert
DESIGN FIRM
Cullinane Design
DESIGNER
Jenn Perman

CLIENT
Sony Pictures Entertainment
DESIGN FIRM
Evenson Design Group
DESIGNERS
Mark Sojka, Brent Jacobson,
Stan Evenson, Christiane Friess

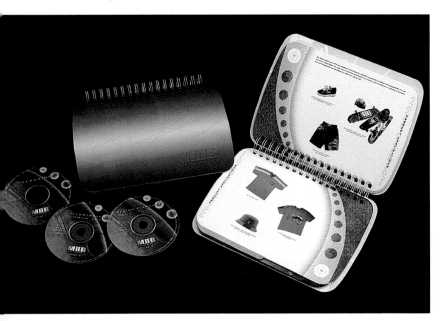

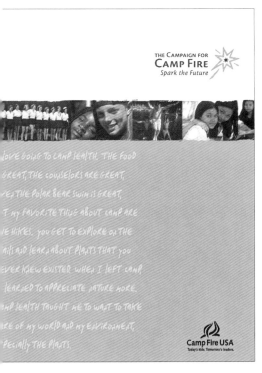

CLIENT
  Campfire USA Central Puget Sound
DESIGN FIRM
  Belyea
DESIGNER
  Anne Dougherty

CLIENT
  Tree Top
DESIGN FIRM
  Hornall Anderson Design Works, Inc.
DESIGNERS
  Katha Dalton, Jana Nishi,
  Michael Brugman

CLIENT
  Bayer Corporation, Diagnostics
DESIGN FIRM
  Hadtke Associates
DESIGNER
  KC Toh

The World's Leading Granite, Direct From The Quarry

CLIENT
Erickson McGovern
DESIGN FIRM
Hornall Anderson Design Works, Inc.
DESIGNERS
Jack Anderson, Kathy Saito,
Henry Yiu

CLIENT
Rock of Ages
DESIGN FIRM
The Imagination Company
DESIGNERS
Jim Giberti, John Turner

CLIENT
The Children's Legacy
DESIGN FIRM
Asher Studio
DESIGNERS
Connie Asher,
Russ Chilcoat

CLIENT
Diocese of Pittsburgh Foundation
DESIGN FIRM
Sewickley Graphics & Design, Inc.
DESIGNER
Michael Seidl

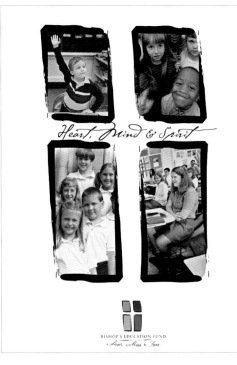

LOOK AT US.

CLIENT
  MaryGrove College
DESIGN FIRM
  Premier Communications Group
DESIGNERS
  Randy Fossano, Pete Pultz,
  Patrick Hatfield

CLIENT
  Weyerhaeuser Realty Investor (WRI)
DESIGN FIRM
  Hornall Anderson Design Works, Inc.
DESIGNERS
  Jack Anderson, James Tee,
  Gretchen Cook, Elmer dela Cruz,
  Jana Nishi

CLIENT
  Wausau Papers
DESIGN FIRM
  Larsen Design + Interactive
DESIGNERS
  Paul Wharton, Bill Pflipsen,
  Pam E. Powell

CLIENT
  MasterCard/Maestro
DESIGN FIRM
  The Dave and Alex Show
DESIGNERS
  Tracie Lissauer, Dave Goldenberg,
  Alexander Isley

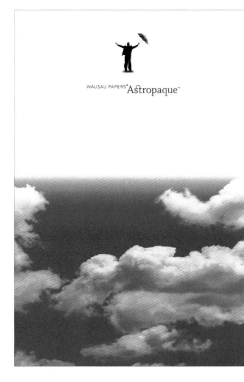

Authorized Signature   Not Valid Unless Signed

The Banking Card Agreement governs the use of this card. It may only be used
by the person to whom it was issued. This card is property of the issuer and must
be returned to the associated bank upon demand.

For 24-hour customer service call: 1-800-555-3572.

et sizes and easier cash management.

Maestro® provides you with a
fast and reliable alternative for
processing your merchants' PIN
debit transactions. And all at an
attractive cost per transaction.

With the strength
of MasterCard
behind it, Maestro
helps your business
by helping your
customers.
Add it to your
offerings today.

- Already welcomed at over 5.4
  million merchant locations.

- The unsurpassed network
  availability and transaction
  approval you've come to expect
  from the MasterCard family
  of brands.

- Multi-site processing gives Maestro
  redundant processing and disaster
  recovery capabilities.

- Low per-transaction costs give
  you a competitive advantage over
  other routing choices.

- Free Maestro signage saves
  you money.

Maestro. Customers carry it.
Merchants want it. Shouldn't you
offer it? Call 1-914-249-6111 today
and discover the value of Maestro.

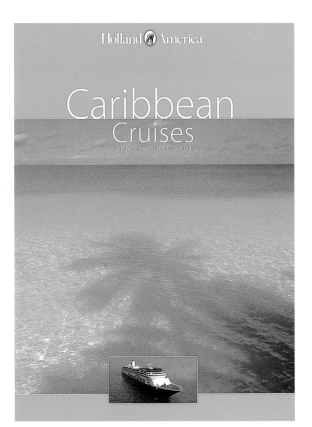

CLIENT
  Holland America Line
DESIGN FIRM
  Hornall Anderson Design Works, Inc.
DESIGNERS
  John Hornall, Julie Lock, Jana Nishi,
  Mary Chin Hutchison, Jana Wilson Esser,
  Mary Hermes, Jeff Wolf, Tiffany Scheiblauer

CLIENT
  Nexen
DESIGN FIRM
  Larsen Design + Interactive
DESIGNERS
  Jo Davison, Bill Pflipsen,
  Pam E. Powell

CLIENT
  Associated Reporters
DESIGN FIRM
  Brand, Ltd.
DESIGNER
  Virginia Thompson Martino

HOSPITALITY The Art of Accommodation

Architecture of the hotel should capture the unique quality of the location of the property. In addition, the design and interior decor of the room should create an atmosphere that communicates a similar sense of place.

Architecture | Planning | Interior Design | The Stubbins Associates, Inc.   TSA of Nevada LLP

[FastFunds]

[money on the move]

CLIENT
  Fast Funds
DESIGN FIRM
  Brad Norr Design
DESIGNER
  Brad D. Norr

CLIENT
  The Stubbins Associates, Inc.
DESIGN FIRM
  Nassar Design
DESIGNERS
  Nelida Nassar,
  Margarita Enconienda

CLIENT
  Maxtor
DESIGN FIRM
  Hornall Anderson Design Works, Inc.
DESIGNERS
  Lisa Cerveny,
  Andrew Wicklund

CLIENT
  Georgia Merit System
DESIGN FIRM
  Jones Worley Design Inc.
DESIGNER
  Michael Sater

Maxtor

2001 MAXTOR ANNUAL REPORT

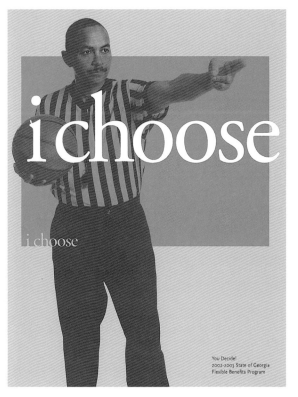

ichoose

i choose

You Decide!
2002-2003 State of Georgia
Flexible Benefits Program

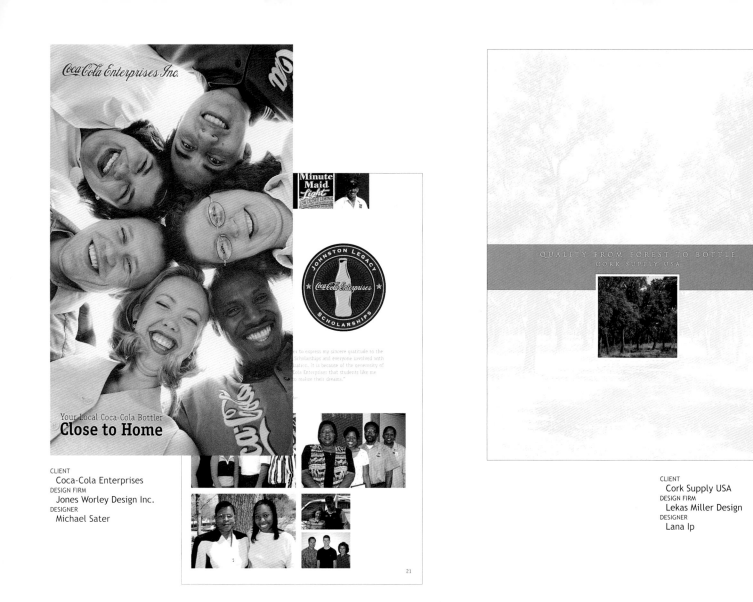

CLIENT
Coca-Cola Enterprises
DESIGN FIRM
Jones Worley Design Inc.
DESIGNER
Michael Sater

CLIENT
Cork Supply USA
DESIGN FIRM
Lekas Miller Design
DESIGNER
Lana Ip

CLIENT
Target
DESIGN FIRM
Graphiculture
DESIGNER
Cheryl Watson

CLIENT
National Zoological Park
DESIGN FIRM
Grafik
DESIGNERS
Kristin Goetz, Judy Kirpich,
Alysia Orrel, Lynn Umemoto

Smithsonian
National Zoological Park

Meeting the Challenge
of Preserving Global
Biodiversity

through
Reproductive
Science

The Animals

CLIENT
Special Start Academy
DESIGN FIRM
Pressley Jacobs
DESIGNER
Patrick Schab

SPECIAL**START**ACADEMY

there is a place for me

►6

Smithsonian
National Zoological Park

FALL
2002

M|C
MICHELE CAULEYS SALON

CLIENT
M.C. Salon
DESIGN FIRM
Design Coup
DESIGNER
Michael Higgins

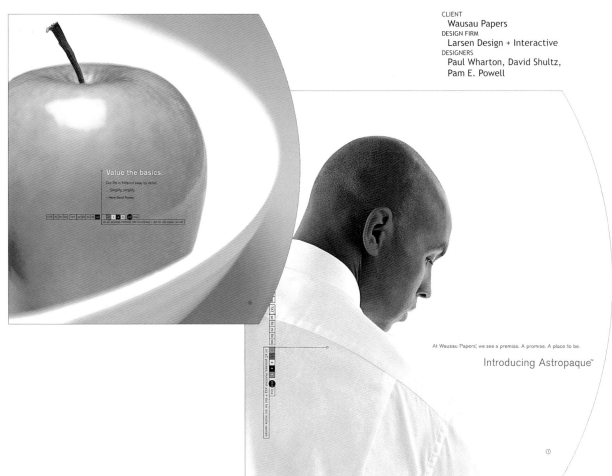

CLIENT
Wausau Papers
DESIGN FIRM
Larsen Design + Interactive
DESIGNERS
**Paul Wharton, David Shultz,
Pam E. Powell**

Value the basics.

Our life is frittered away by detail.
...Simplify, simplify.
—Henry David Thoreau

At Wausau Papers, we see a premise. A promise. A place to be.

Introducing Astropaque™

CLIENT
Appropriate Temporaries, Inc.
DESIGN FIRM
The Leyo Group, Inc.
DESIGNER
Jason Turner

Appropriate
Temporaries

CLIENT
Cadillac Motor
DESIGN FIRM
Iconix, Inc.
DESIGNER
Mary Kay Gill

2004 CADILLAC SRX

INVIGORAT **I □ N**

The **I □ N** is designed to excite young buyers with its
combination of leading standard horsepower,
sporty handling and contemporary features,
like the center mounted instrument cluster.

I □ N | Quad Coupe and Sedan

CLIENT
General Motors—Saturn
DESIGN FIRM
Iconix, Inc.
DESIGNER
Susan Boucher

CLIENT
Stratos
DESIGN FIRM
Platform Creative Group
DESIGNER
Kathy Thompson

CLIENT
Herman Miller Inc.
DESIGN FIRM
Herman Miller Inc.
DESIGNERS
Brian Edlefson,
Sharon Boehm

S T R A T O S
creativity engineered

Stratos Product Development, LLC

design   engineering   marketing   incubation   www.stratos.com

What is Herman Miller?

An Introduction to the Herman Miller Brand

CLIENT
FreeMotion
DESIGN FIRM
Hornall Anderson Design Works, Inc.
DESIGNERS
Jack Anderson, Kathy Saito,
Sonja Max, Henry Yiu, Alan Copeland

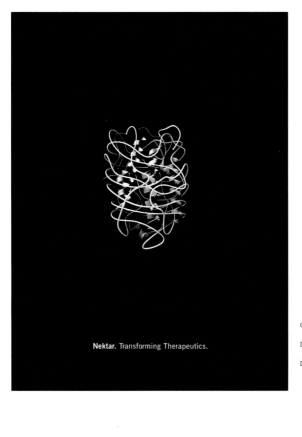

Nektar. Transforming Therapeutics.

CLIENT
Nektar Therapeutics
DESIGN FIRM
Cahan & Associates
DESIGNERS
Sharrie Brooks,
Bill Cahan

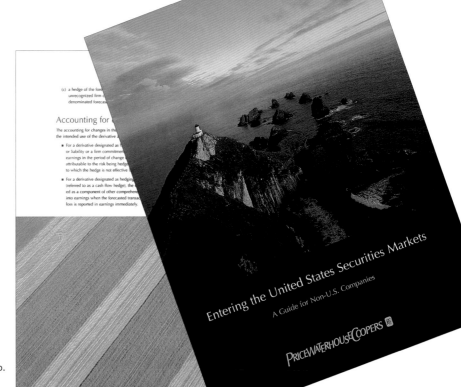

Entering the United States Securities Markets

A Guide for Non-U.S. Companies

PriceWaterhouseCoopers

CLIENT
CFO's & CEO's of Major Global Corp.
DESIGN FIRM
Pricewaterhouse Coopers
DESIGNERS
Raquella Kagaw

CLIENT
Hyper Car
DESIGN FIRM
Schwener Design Group
DESIGNERS
Diane Schwener,
Jen Collier

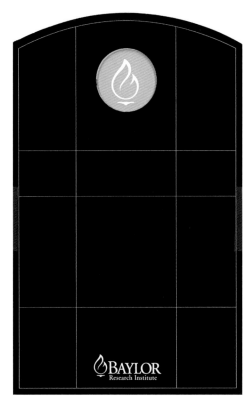

CLIENT
Baylor Health Care System
DESIGN FIRM
DAM Creative, Inc.
DESIGNERS
Dana Meek, Matt Mollet

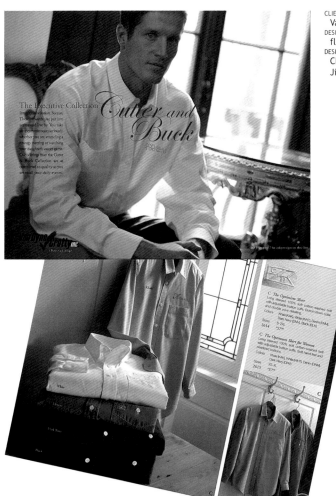

CLIENT
Van Dyne Crotty
DESIGN FIRM
flourish
DESIGNERS
Christopher Ferranti, Charity Ewanko,
Jing Lauengco

CLIENT
Zoe
DESIGN FIRM
Cahan & Associates
DESIGNERS
Gary Williams,
Bill Cahan

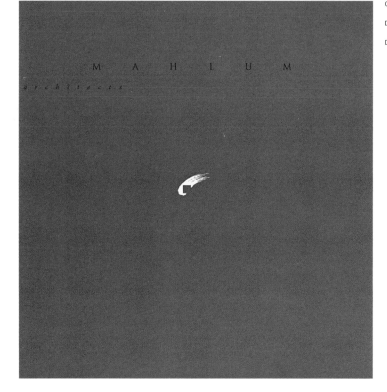

CLIENT
Mahlum Architects
DESIGN FIRM
Hornall Anderson Design Works, Inc.
DESIGNERS
Jack Anderson, Kathy Saito,
Sonja Max, Henry Yiu, Alan Copeland

CLIENT
Line & Tone
DESIGN FIRM
Notovitz Communications

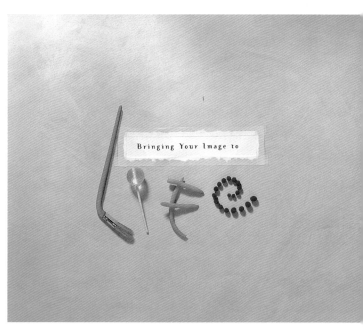

CLIENT
Dever Designs
DESIGN FIRM
Dever Designs
DESIGNER
Jeffrey L. Dever

LOGOS

CLIENT
Skymedia Airships
DESIGN FIRM
Hetz Advertising
DESIGNER
Michael Hetz

SKYMEDIA AIRSHIPS

CLIENT
Dunkin' Donuts
DESIGN FIRM
Hill Holliday
DESIGNER
Mina Kalemkeryan

CLIENT
Office of The Governor Jesse Ventura
DESIGN FIRM
Capsule
DESIGNER
Brian Adducci

JACKAL|OPEN
the governor's fall golf classic

CLIENT
DFI International
DESIGN FIRM
Sightline Marketing
DESIGNERS
Clay Marshaall,
Samantha Guerry

DFI INTERNATIONAL

CLIENT
Dirty Olive Martini Kit
DESIGN FIRM
Portfolio Center
DESIGNER
Louis Bravo

CLIENT
PhotonLight.com
DESIGN FIRM
Defteling Design
DESIGNER
Alex Wijnen

PHOTON|Light.COM

CLIENT
Event Pros, Inc.
DESIGN FIRM
Indicia Design, Inc.
DESIGNER
Ryan Hembree

CLIENT
Rhythm Deluxe—Blues Band
DESIGN FIRM
Never Boring Design
DESIGNERS
Melody MacMurray,
David Boring

CLIENT
GlaxoSmithKline
DESIGNER
Paul Barlow

CLIENT
Linear Logic, Inc.
DESIGN FIRM
Premier Communications Group
DESIGNER
Joe Becker

CLIENT
Stanford Center for Innovations in Learning
DESIGN FIRM
Meta Design
DESIGNERS
Brett Wickens,
Patrick Au-Yeung

CLIENT
Bring
DESIGN FIRM
Funk/Levis & Associates
DESIGNER
David Funk

CLIENT
Philly Grill
DESIGN FIRM
Funk/Levis & Associates
DESIGNER
Jason Anderson

CLIENT
Batch Beverages
DESIGN FIRM
Out Of The Box
DESIGNER
Rick Schneider

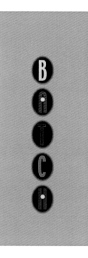

CLIENT
Spinnaker Networks
DESIGN FIRM
Kolano Design
DESIGNER
Cate Sides

S P I N N A K E R
N E T W O R K S

CLIENT
Brown University
DESIGN FIRM
Gill Fishman Associates
DESIGNERS
Alicia Ozyjowski,
Gill Fishman

[cac]

CLIENT
RTKL
DESIGN FIRM
ID8 Studio/RTKL
DESIGNER
Don Roy

RTKL DESIGN CONFERENCE

CLIENT
Harvard University
DESIGN FIRM
Gill Fishman Associates
DESIGNERS
Alicia Ozyjowski
Gill Fishman

ves.

CLIENT
Marketing Section
DESIGN FIRM
Bremmer & Goris Communications
DESIGNER
Dennis Goris

THE MARKETING SECTION

Marketing Talent for the Legal Profession

CLIENT
Atlantic Long—Term Care
Insurance Agency
DESIGN FIRM
Ted DeCagna Graphic Design
DESIGNER
Ted DeCagna

Atlantic Long-Term Care
Insurance Agency

CLIENT
Riverside Financial Group
DESIGN FIRM
Ted DeCagna Graphic Design
DESIGNER
Ted DeCagna Graphic Design

CLIENT
Simpson & Brown Marine and
Land Construction
DESIGN FIRM
Ted DeCagma Graphic Design
DESIGNER
Ted DeCagna

CLIENT
McKnight Property Management
DESIGN FIRM
Kolano Design
DESIGNEP
Timothy Carrera

NORTHLAND
HEALTH CENTER

CLIENT
I-Proof
DESIGN FIRM
Ridge Creative
DESIGNERS
Jeanna Pool, David Coleman

proof

CLIENT
Aquea Design
DESIGN FIRM
Aquea Design
DESIGNER
Raymond Perez

AQUEA
GRAPHIC DESIGN

CLIENT
Grant Architects
DESIGN FIRM
Kolano Design
DESIGNER
Adrienne Ciuprinskas

GRANT ARCHITECTS

CLIENT
Faribault Foods
DESIGN FIRM
Hillis Design
DESIGNERS
Anna Clark,
John Hillis

Faríbault Foods

CLIENT
Media Directions
DESIGN FIRM
McKnight Kurland Baccelli

MEDIA DIRECTIONS

CLIENT
Keyes & Toraason Dental
Associates, Ltd.
DESIGN FIRM
The Leyo Group, Inc.
DESIGNERS
Horst Mickler,
Mike Kelly

CLIENT
Geoffrey's Malibu Restaurant
DESIGN FIRM
Blinn Design
DESIGNER
K.C. Blinn

GEOFFREY'S · MALIBU

CLIENT
West Coast Aquatics
DESIGN FIRM
Hornall Anderson Design Works, Inc.
DESIGNERS
Jack Anderson,
Sonja Max

WEST COAST AQUATICS

CLIENT
Cleveland Indians
DESIGN FIRM
Herip Associates
DESIGNERS
Walter M. Herip,
John R. Menter

CLIENT
Visser Health Care Products
DESIGN FIRM
Holly Dickens Design
DESIGNER
Holly Dickens

Wild Medicine

CLIENT
Multivision Design
DESIGN FIRM
Multivision Design
DESIGNERS
Rick Gutierrez,
Netz Gomez

multiVision design

a strategic marketing design company

CLIENT
The Sutton Group/
North General Hospital (NYC)
DESIGN FIRM
Design Nut
DESIGNER
Brent M. Almond

N
NORTH GENERAL
H O S P I T A L

Growing With Our Community, Caring For Your Health

CLIENT
LiveScore.com
DESIGN FIRM
MFDI
DESIGNER
Mark Fertig

CLIENT
Cuyahoga Valley
National Park
DESIGN FIRM
Herip Associates
DESIGNERS
Walter M. Herip,
John R. Menter

Cuyahoga Valley

Countryside
Conservancy

CLIENT
European Capital Ventures
DESIGN FIRM
Magical Monkey
DESIGNER
Roswitha Rodriques

EUROPEAN**CAPITAL**VENTURES NV
ECV

CLIENT
Harvard
DESIGN FIRM
Phoenix Design Works
DESIGNER
James M. Skiles

HARVARD

CLIENT
Americans for the Arts
DESIGN FIRM
FUSZION Collaborative
DESIGNER
John Foster

CLIENT
National Pro Fast Pitch
DESIGN FIRM
Rassman Design
DESIGNERS
Glen Hobbs,
John Rassman

CLIENT
Coca-Cola Hydration Business Unit
DESIGN FIRM
Finished Art, Inc.
DESIGNERS
Kannex Fung,
Ake Nimsuwan

CLIENT
U.S. Parks Department
DESIGN FIRM
Stephen Longo
Design Assoc.
DESIGNER
Stephen Longo

CLIENT
Block Consulting
DESIGN FIRM
Bruce Yelaska Design
DESIGNER
Bruce Yelaska

BLOCK CONSULTING

CLIENT
Osaka Sushi Bar
DESIGN FIRM
m3ad.com
DESIGNER
Dan McElhattan III

CLIENT
Steel City Media
DESIGN FIRM
Kolano Design
DESIGNER
Adrienne Ciuprinskas

LA STRADA
DOWNTOWN

CLIENT
Mark V. Martino,
Virginia Thompson Martino
DESIGN FIRM
Brand, Ltd.
DESIGNERS
Mark V. Martino,
Virginia Thompson Martino

CLIENT
Communitools
DESIGN FIRM
MFDI
DESIGNER
Mark Fertig

CLIENT
Achillion Pharmaceuticals
DESIGN FIRM
Taylor Design
DESIGNERS
Steve Habersang,
Daniel Taylor,
Matt Laverty

CLIENT
Rule29
DESIGN FIRM
Rule29
DESIGNER
Justin Ahrens

CLIENT
The City of Jacksonville
DESIGN FIRM
HardBall Sports
DESIGNER
Michael O'Connell

CLIENT
David H. Smith Fellows
DESIGN FIRM
FUSZION Collaborative
DESIGNER
John Foster

CLIENT
Susan Schoen LMT CNMT
DESIGN FIRM
Gouthier Design
DESIGNERS
Kiley Del Valle,
Jonathan Gouthier

CLIENT
MLBP
DESIGN FIRM
Phoenix Design Works
DESIGNER
James M. Skiles

CLIENT
Valles Caldera Trust/
USDA Forest Service
DESIGN FIRM
Jeff Fisher LogoMotives
DESIGNER
Jeff Fisher

CLIENT
The Soaring Spirit, Inc.
DESIGN FIRM
Arnold/Ostrom Advertising
DESIGNERS
Cara Albrecht,
Jacqueline Hoopman

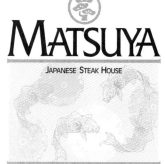

CLIENT
2 Girls & a Trunk
DESIGN FIRM
Studio Graphique
DESIGNER
Gina Gerken

CLIENT
Asparagus Media
DESIGN FIRM
Gecko Creative
DESIGNER
Matthew Rowland

CLIENT
Denver Young Artists Orchestra
DESIGN FIRM
Rassman Design
DESIGNERS
Glen Hobbs,
John Rassman

CLIENT
Matsuya
DESIGN FIRM
Stephen Longo
Design Assoc.
DESIGNER
Stephen Longo

CLIENT
Zullo Communications
DESIGN FIRM
Bonato Design
DESIGNERS
Donna Bonato,
Robin Bonato

CLIENT
St. Richard's School
DESIGN FIRM
Stahl Partners Inc.
DESIGNER
David Stahl

242 • ACI 2004

JOIN**CA**
go to **ca**.**com**

BUILDING
ON
FAITH

Santa Barbara

7WEST

connexstar℠
by Spacenet

STANDING
UNITED

CLIENT
Vein Clinics of America
DESIGN FIRM
Crowley Webb and Associates
DESIGNER
Kelly Gambino

CLIENT
MBA Management
DESIGN FIRM
Phoenix Creative Group
DESIGNER
Angela Buchanico

CLIENT
Music For The World
DESIGN FIRM
Toolbox Studios, Inc.
DESIGNERS
Paul Soupiset,
Ryan Foerster

CLIENT
Four Points Architectural Services
DESIGN FIRM
Minx Design
DESIGNER
Cecilia M. Sveda

CLIENT
Atlantic Insurance
DESIGN FIRM
Nordyke Design
DESIGNER
John Nordyke

CLIENT
Meditech Health Services, Inc.
DESIGN FIRM
Barbara Brown
Marketing & Design
DESIGNERS
Barbara Brown,
Jon A. Leslie

CLIENT
Comedicus, Inc.
DESIGN FIRM
Arnold/Ostrom Advertising
DESIGNER
Jacqueline Hoopman

CLIENT
Dun & Bradstreet
DESIGN FIRM
Studio Graphique
DESIGNER
Gina Gerken

CLIENT
Tib's Louisiana Grill
DESIGN FIRM
Berry Design, Inc.
DESIGNERS
Bob Berry,
Rob Zides

CLIENT
Barnes & Noble
DESIGN FIRM
Red Canoe
DESIGNERS
Deb Koch,
Caroline Kavanagh

BARNES & NOBLE digital

CLIENT
NBAP
DESIGN FIRM
Phoenix Design Works
DESIGNER
James M. Skiles

CLIENT
Architecture Office David Krebs
DESIGN FIRM
flourish
DESIGNERS
Christopher Ferranti,
Steve Shuman,
Jing Lauengco,
Justin Campbell

a°dk

CLIENT
Sunrise Brand
DESIGN FIRM
Holly Dickens Design
DESIGNER
Holly Dickens

CLIENT
Triad Hospital Corporation
DESIGN FIRM
GCG Advertising
DESIGNER
Brian Wilburn

MESA VIEW
REGIONAL HOSPITAL

CLIENT
Academy Bridge to Moorpark College
DESIGN FIRM
Barbara Brown
Marketing & Design
DESIGNERS
Barbara Brown,
Alicia Hoskins

ACADEMY BRIDGE
TO MOORPARK COLLEGE

CLIENT
Kuester Enterprises Inc.
DESIGN FIRM
Stahl Partners Inc.
DESIGNER
David Stahl

SEGCO™

CLIENT
Gregg Primm
DESIGN FIRM
M3ad.com
DESIGNER
Dan McElhattan III

CLIENT
Cuyahoga Valley
National Park
DESIGN FIRM
Herip Associates
DESIGNERS
Walter M. Herip,
John R. Menter

CLIENT
GoodSports
DESIGN FIRM
TJ Chameleon Graphic Communications
DESIGNER
Richard Berry

CLIENT
Indianapolis 500
DESIGN FIRM
Phoenix Design Works
DESIGNER
James M. Skiles

CLIENT
Holly Dickens Design
DESIGN FIRM
Holly Dickens Design
DESIGNER
Holly Dickens

CLIENT
Zeke's Smokehouse
DESIGN FIRM
Sargent & Berman
DESIGNERS
Peter Sargent,
Barbara Chan

CLIENT
NorGlobe
DESIGN FIRM
Design Nut
DESIGNER
Brent M. Almond

CLIENT
Saarman Construction
DESIGN FIRM
Bruce Yelaska Design
DESIGNER
Bruce Yelaska

CLIENT
  An Encyclopedia of Gay, Lesbian, Bisexual,
  Transgender & Queer Culture
DESIGN FIRM
  Top Design Studio
DESIGNERS
  Rebekah Beaton,
  Peleg Top

CLIENT
  Sicura
DESIGNER
  Gorete Ferreira

SICURA

CLIENT
  Nirchel Exports
DESIGN FIRM
  Magical Monkey
DESIGNER
  Roswitha Rodriques

Nirchel E^Xports LLC

CLIENT
  Progressive Viticulture
DESIGN FIRM
  Marcia Herrmann Design
DESIGNER
  Marcia Herrmann

PROGRESSIVE
VITICULTURE

CLIENT
  Computer Associates
DESIGN FIRM
  CA in house
  Creative Development Dept.
DESIGNER
  Loren Moss Meyer

CLIENT
  ivia network, Inc.
DESIGN FIRM
  Conry Design
DESIGNER
  Rhonda Conry

CLIENT
  Long Island Center for Business &
  Professional Women
DESIGN FIRM
  Guarino Graphics
  & Design Studio
DESIGNER
  Jan Guarino

WELLNESS DAY

CLIENT
  Louisiana State University
DESIGN FIRM
  Phoenix Design Works
DESIGNERS
  James M. Skiles,
  Rod Ollerenshaw,
  Craig Miller,
  Richard Tsai

CLIENT
  Fox Learning Systems
DESIGN FIRM
  Desbrow
DESIGNER
  Brian Lee Campbell

CLIENT
  Tools for Decision
DESIGN FIRM
  The Wecker Group
DESIGNER
  Robert Wecker

CLIENT
  Waterpik Technologies
DESIGN FIRM
  Source/Inc.
DESIGNER
  Adrienne Nole

CLIENT
  World Events Forum
DESIGN FIRM
  The Leyo Group, Inc.
DESIGNERS
  Mike Kelly,
  Horst Mickler

CLIENT
  Green Bay Packers
DESIGN FIRM
  ZD Studios, Inc.
DESIGNERS
  Mark Schmitz,
  Tina Remy

CLIENT
  Burnes Group
DESIGN FIRM
  Source/Inc.
DESIGNER
  Adrienne Nole

CLIENT
  Thunderbox
DESIGN FIRM
  Phoenix Design Works
DESIGNERS
  James M. Skiles

CLIENT
NBAP
DESIGN FIRM
Phoenix Design Works
DESIGNER
James M. Skiles

CLIENT
In The Hunt Farm
DESIGN FIRM
Hubbell Design Works
DESIGNER
Leighton Hubbell

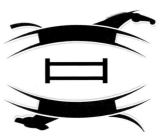

CLIENT
Intelec Group
DESIGN FIRM
Walsh Design
DESIGNER
Miriam Lisco

CLIENT
Pixeltone
DESIGN FIRM
Magical Monkey
DESIGNER
Roswitha Rodrigues

CLIENT
PistonGear
DESIGN FIRM
Christopher Gorz Design
DESIGNER
Chris Gorz

CLIENT
Owl Bay Publishers
DESIGN FIRM
Ray Dugas Design
DESIGNERS
Ross Heck,
Ray B. Dugas

CLIENT
Kraft
DESIGN FIRM
Holly Dickens Design
DESIGNER
Holly Dickens

CLIENT
MLBP
DESIGN FIRM
Phoenix Design Works
DESIGNER
James M. Skiles

CLIENT
Dragonsleaf
DESIGN FIRM
Chen Design Associates
DESIGNER
Leon Yu

CLIENT
Goodbaker
DESIGN FIRM
Lee Busch Design Inc.
DESIGNER
Lee Busch

CLIENT
Praxis
DESIGN FIRM
Crowley Webb and Associates
DESIGNER
Steve Kull

CLIENT
Lance Armstrong Foundation
DESIGN FIRM
Bremmer & Goris Communications
DESIGNER
Dennis Goris

CLIENT
Department of Alcohol and Drug Prevention
DESIGN FIRM
Lawrence & Ponder Ideaworks
DESIGNERS
Jim Bell, Bil Dicks, Maruie Blair,
Gary Frederickson, Cristina Bogossian,
Lynda Lawrence

FACTS DON'T LIE.

CLIENT
Swift & Company
DESIGN FIRM
Rassman Design
DESIGNERS
Lyn D'Amato,
John Rassman

CLIENT
Stark Enterprises, Pepper Pike, OH
DESIGN FIRM
CommArts
DESIGNER
Keith Harley

CROCKER PARK
WESTLAKE

CLIENT
ArtInteractive
DESIGN FIRM
Bottlecap Studios
DESIGNERS
Aimee Goodwin,
Jon Gleasman

ART
INTERACTIVE

CLIENT
MLBP
DESIGN FIRM
Phoenix Design Works
DESIGNER
James M. Skiles

CLIENT
J.M. Clayton Company
DESIGN FIRM
Whitney Edwards Design
DESIGNER
Charlene Whitney Edwards

CLIENT
Aetna
DESIGN FIRM
Bailey Design Group
DESIGNER
Bob Fueinato, Dave Fiedler

CLIENT
Show Intelligence Software
DESIGN FIRM
Karl Kromer Design
DESIGNER
Karl Kromer

CLIENT
The Arts Council
DESIGN FIRM
Insight Design Communications
DESIGNER
Tracy Holdeman

CLIENT
Vision Concepts
DESIGN FIRM
Ray Dugas Design
DESIGNER
Ray B. Dugas

CLIENT
Digital Signage Solutions
DESIGN FIRM
Kolano Design
DESIGNER
Cate Sides

CLIENT
Fannie Mae
DESIGN FIRM
Graves Fowler Associates
DESIGNER
Victoria Q. Robinson

CLIENT
Mass Energy Alliance
DESIGN FIRM
O'Sullivan Communications
DESIGNER
Cheryl Allen

CLIENT
Caribbean Latin American Action
DESIGN FIRM
Octavo Designs
DESIGNER
Mark Burrier

m a

mass energy alliance

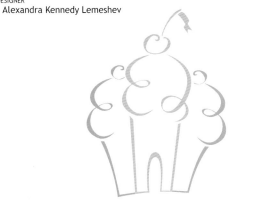

CLIENT
McGuire Co.
DESIGN FIRM
Holly Dickens Design
DESIGNER
Holly Dickens

CLIENT
Kings and Sages Apparel
DESIGNER
Alexandra Kennedy Lemeshev

610 Clematis

Ice Cream Castles

CLIENT
Trade Capture
DESIGN FIRM
Taylor Design
DESIGNERS
Hannah Fichandler,
Dan Taylor

CLIENT
Stephen Longo
DESIGN FIRM
Stephen Longo Design Assoc.
DESIGNER
Stephen Longo

ICTS Symphony

STEPHEN LONGO DESIGN ASSOCIATES

CLIENT
Palermo's
DESIGN FIRM
Design North, Inc.
DESIGNER
Pat Cowen

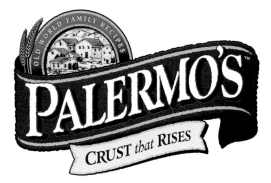

CLIENT
MLS
DESIGN FIRM
Phoenix Design Works
DESIGNER
James M. Skiles

CLIENT
Amino Entertainment
DESIGN FIRM
Peñabrand/Butler, Shine & Stern
DESIGNER
Luis Peña

CLIENT
Frank Frasier Design
DESIGN FIRM
Phoenix Design Works
DESIGNERS
James M. Skiles,
Rod Ollerenshaw

CLIENT
Robert Wood Johnson Foundation
DESIGN FIRM
Graves Fowler Associates
DESIGNER
Kristin Braaten

CLIENT
Old Orchard Brands
DESIGN FIRM
Bailey Design Group
DESIGNERS
Steve Perry,
Dave Fiedler

CLIENT
  M&P Design Group
DESIGN FIRM
  McElveney & Palozzi Design Group
DESIGNERS
  Lisa Williamson,
  Jon Westfall

CLIENT
  Vascular Health Institute
DESIGN FIRM
  Stahl Partners Inc.
DESIGNERS
  David Stahl,
  Brian Gray

CLIENT
  Ken Shamblen, Kinexsis
DESIGN FIRM
  Milestone Design, Inc.
DESIGNER
  Diane Gianfagna-Meil

CLIENT
  BG Products
DESIGN FIRM
  Insight Design Communications
DESIGNER
  Tracy Holdeman

CLIENT
  Walsh Design
DESIGN FIRM
  Walsh Design
DESIGNER
  Miriam Lisco

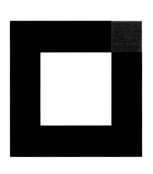

CLIENT
  Atascadero Chamber of Commerce
DESIGN FIRM
  Pierre Rademaker Design
DESIGNERS
  Pierre Rademaker, Debbie Shibata

CLIENT
Louisiana State University
DESIGN FIRM
Phoenix Design Works
DESIGNERS
James M. Skiles, Rod Ollerenshaw,
Craig Miller, Richard Tsai

CLIENT
Gifttrends.com
DESIGN FIRM
Karl Kromer Design
DESIGNER
Karl Kromer

CLIENT
Meijer
DESIGN FIRM
InGear
DESIGNER
Matt Hassler

CLIENT
Pixeltone
DESIGN FIRM
Magical Monkey
DESIGNER
Roswitha Rodrigues

CLIENT
Gravity Post
DESIGN FIRM
Hubbell Design Works
DESIGNER
Leighton Hubbell

CLIENT
Invent.com
DESIGN FIRM
MFDI
DESIGNER
Mark Fertig

BOX.COM

CLIENT
Anarumo-Zoar Realty Inc.
DESIGN FIRM
Guarino Graphics & Design Studio
DESIGNER
Jan Guarino

CLIENT
Palisades Realty
DESIGN FIRM
Kiku Obata + Company
DESIGNER
Todd Mayberry

CLIENT
Amtrak
DESIGN FIRM
Bremmer & Goris Communications
DESIGNERS
Dennis Goris

CLIENT
Robert Wood Johnson Foundation
DESIGN FIRM
Graves Fowler Associates
DESIGNER
Kristin Braaten

Building
Community Supports
for Diabetes Care

CLIENT
IT-GEO, Division of Edinfor
DESIGN FIRM
Gage Design
DESIGNER
Chris Roberts

CLIENT
Wonderworks Exhibits
DESIGN FIRM
Capt Flynn Advertising
DESIGNERS
Tom Rigsby, Isaac Munoz

CLIENT
Cairns + Associates
DESIGN FIRM
Cairns + Associates
DESIGNER
Ethan Ries

CAIRNS + ASSOCIATES

CLIENT
Centage Corporation
DESIGN FIRM
Lee Busch Design Inc.
DESIGNER
Lee Busch

centage™

CLIENT
Touchworx Inc.
DESIGN FIRM
Whistle
DESIGNER
Rory Carlton

TOUCH
WORX

CLIENT
Datatel
DESIGN FIRM
Bremmer & Goris Communications
DESIGNER
Fred Flerlage

THE
CENTER FOR INSTITUTIONAL
EFFECTIVENESS™

CLIENT
Neura Baked
DESIGN FIRM
Holly Dickens Design
DESIGNER
Holly Dickens

NEURA
BAKED

CLIENT
State Capital Global Law Firm Group
DESIGN FIRM
Greenfield/Belser Ltd.
DESIGNERS
Burkey Belser, John Bruns

STATE CAPITAL
GLOBAL LAW FIRM GROUP

CLIENT
EastBanc
DESIGN FIRM
Grafix
DESIGNERS
Michelle Mar, Lynn Umemoto

CLIENT
Jeff Kroop Inc.
DESIGN FIRM
Gouthier Design
DESIGNERS
Jonathan Gouthier,
Mami Awamura

CLIENT
Vocollect
DESIGN FIRM
Desbrow
DESIGNER
Brian Lee Campbell

CLIENT
Encompass International
DESIGN FIRM
Monster Design
DESIGNER
Denise Sakaki

CLIENT
N.Y. Opera News
DESIGN FIRM
Holly Dickens Design
DESIGNER
Holly Dickens

CLIENT
Milestone Properties
DESIGN FIRM
Genghis Design
DESIGNER
Dale Monahan

CLIENT
NBAP
DESIGN FIRM
Phoenix Design Works
DESIGNER
James M. Skiles

CLIENT
MLBP
DESIGN FIRM
Phoenix Design Works
DESIGNER
James M. Skiles

CLIENT
SSOE
DESIGN FIRM
Phoenix Design Works
DESIGNERS
James M. Skiles, Rod Ollerenshaw

CLIENT
Coca-Cola Companies
DESIGN FIRM
Phoenix Design Works
DESIGNERS
James M. Skiles,
Rod Ollerenshaw

CLIENT
Breeders' Cup
DESIGN FIRM
Phoenix Design Works
DESIGNERS
James M. Skiles,
Rod Ollerenshaw,
Craig Miller,
Richard Tsai

CLIENT
Jaguar
DESIGN FIRM
Phoenix Design Works
DESIGNERS
James M. Skiles,
Rod Ollerenshaw

CLIENT
MLBP
DESIGN FIRM
Phoenix Design Works
DESIGNER
James M. Skiles

CLIENT
Brown University
DESIGN FIRM
Phoenix Design Works
DESIGNER
James M. Skiles

CLIENT
ESPN Magazine
DESIGN FIRM
Phoenix Design Works
DESIGNERS
James M. Skiles, Rod Ollerenshaw

CLIENT
Walt Disney Companies
DESIGN FIRM
Phoenix Design Works
DESIGNERS
James M. Skiles, Rod Ollerenshaw

CLIENT
Target Corporation
DESIGN FIRM
Wink/Target Advertising
DESIGNER
Scott Thares/Wink

CLIENT
NBAP
DESIGN FIRM
Phoenix Design Works
DESIGNER
James M. Skiles

CLIENT
Vietnam Veterans Memorial Fund
DESIGN FIRM
Bremmer & Goris Communications
DESIGNER
Fred Flerlage

CLIENT
Crowell & Moring
DESIGN FIRM
Bremmer & Goris Communications
DESIGNER
Fred Flerlage

VIETNAM VETERANS MEMORIAL FUND

crowell moring

Your guide to the top.

CLIENT
Waukegan Savings & Loan
DESIGN FIRM
Anna Ohalla, Inc.
DESIGNER
Anna Ohalla

CLIENT
Life & Health of America
DESIGN FIRM
Bailey Design Group
DESIGNERS
Dave Fiedler, Jerry Corcoran

Waukegan
Savings

LIFE & HEALTH of AMERICA

CLIENT
IQ Navigator
DESIGN FIRM
Rassman Design
DESIGNERS
Glen Hobbs, John Rassman

CLIENT
Parallax Ventures, Inc.
DESIGN FIRM
Barbara Brown Marketing & Design
DESIGNERS
Barbara Brown, Jon A. Leslie

IQNavigator

PARALLAX
VENTURES, INC.

CLIENT
MLBP
DESIGN FIRM
Phoenix Design Works
DESIGNER
James M. Skiles

CLIENT
Martin Resorts
DESIGN FIRM
Pierre Rademaker Design
DESIGNERS
Pierre Rademaker, Debbie Shibata

CLIENT
JetEquity
DESIGN FIRM
Magical Monkey
DESIGNER
Roswitha Rodriques

CLIENT
Guide Dog Ltd.
DESIGN FIRM
New Leaf Publishing, Inc.
DESIGNER
Michelle Morgan Cordle

CLIENT
Greenmachine
DESIGN FIRM
Whistle
DESIGNER
Rory Carlton

CLIENT
Road Kill Canteen
DESIGN FIRM
Octavo Designs
DESIGNER
Eryn Willard

CLIENT
Harvard
DESIGN FIRM
Phoenix Design Works
DESIGNER
James M. Skiles

CLIENT
Show Me Tickets
DESIGN FIRM
MFDI
DESIGNER
Mark Fertig

CLIENT
Mavericks Gym
DESIGN FIRM
Barbara Brown Marketing & Design
DESIGNERS
Barbara Brown, Jon A. Leslie

CLIENT
Center for Contemporary Printmaking
DESIGN FIRM
Lister Butler Consulting
DESIGNERS
John Lister, William Davis

Center for
Contemporary
Printmaking

CLIENT
Cuyahoga Valley National Park
DESIGN FIRM
Herip Associates
DESIGNERS
Walter M. Herip,
John R. Menter

CLIENT
onShore Development
DESIGN FIRM
dawn design
DESIGNER
Dawn Peccatiello

CLIENT
Nobilo Winery
DESIGN FIRM
Full Steam Marketing
DESIGNERS
Liz Nolan,
Eric Jepson

CLIENT
Sonoma State University
DESIGN FIRM
Phoenix Design Works
DESIGNERS
James M. Skiles, Rod Ollerenshaw,
Craig Miller, Richard Tsai

CLIENT
Atlantis
DESIGN FIRM
Holly Dickens Design
DESIGNER
Holly Dickens

CLIENT
Pet Kingdom
DESIGN FIRM
Sayles Graphic Design
DESIGNERS
John Sayles,
Som Inthalangsy

CLIENT
Coca Cola
DESIGN FIRM
Jones Design Group
DESIGNERS
Brody Boyer,
Vicky Jones

CLIENT
Weinsheimer Group
DESIGN FIRM
LekasMiller Design
DESIGNER
Lana Ip

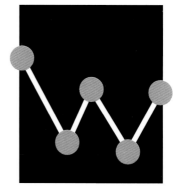

CLIENT
Volunteer Frederick
DESIGN FIRM
Octavo Designs
DESIGNERS
Eryn Willard, Sue Hough

CLIENT
Chinablue, Inc.
DESIGN FIRM
Hubbell Design Works
DESIGNER
Leighton Hubbell

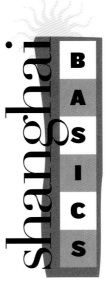

CLIENT
MLBP
DESIGN FIRM
Phoenix Design Works
DESIGNER
James M. Skiles

CLIENT
NEC Mitsubishi Electronics Display
DESIGN FIRM
Liska + Associates, Inc.
DESIGNER
Paul Wong

ClearFlat

CLIENT
Roc Trading
DESIGN FIRM
Karl Kromer Design
DESIGNER
Karl Kromer

ROCTRADING
Electronic Day Trading

CLIENT
Treehouse,Inc.
DESIGN FIRM
Milestone Design, Inc.
DESIGNER
Diane Gianfagna-Meils

CLIENT
  Northland Investment Corporation
DESIGN FIRM
  Greenfield/Belser Ltd
DESIGNER
  Burkey Belser

CLIENT
  Webline Designs
DESIGN FIRM
  Guarino Graphics + Design Studio
DESIGNER
  Jan Guarino

CLIENT
  Boyt
DESIGN FIRM
  Source/Inc.
DESIGNER
  William Harper

CLIENT
  Tenuteq Inc.
DESIGN FIRM
  Whistle
DESIGNER
  Rory Carlton

CLIENT
  Gus Soto Designs
DESIGN FIRM
  Liska + Associates, Inc.
DESIGNER
  Paul Wong

CLIENT
  RainMinder
DESIGN FIRM
  Bremmer & Goris Communications
DESIGNER
  Brandi Phipps

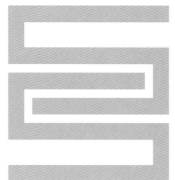

CLIENT
SQA
DESIGN FIRM
Im-aj Communications & Design, Inc.
DESIGNERS
Jami Ouellette, Mark Bevington

SQA | with you every step of the way

CLIENT
Knoll Training
DESIGN FIRM
BBK Studio
DESIGNERS
Brian Hauch, Sharon Oleniczak,
Alison Popp

CLIENT
U.S. Conference of Mayors
DESIGN FIRM
FUSZION Collaborative
DESIGNER
John Foster

CLIENT
Anschutz Entertainment Group
DESIGN FIRM
Hamagami/Carroll
DESIGNER
Justin Carroll

CLIENT
McKenzie Mist
DESIGN FIRM
Poppie Design
DESIGNER
Bill Poppie

CLIENT
Hot Shots in Tabletop
DESIGN FIRM
Bremmer & Goris Communications
DESIGNER
Nicole Haman

HOT SHOTS
IN TABLETOP

The media resource for picture perfect tableware.

CLIENT
Indianapolis 500
DESIGN FIRM
Phoenix Design Works
DESIGNER
James M. Skiles

CLIENT
Triangle Properties
DESIGN FIRM
Guarino Graphics + Design Studio
DESIGNER
Jan Guarino

CLIENT
Palm Beach International Polo Club
DESIGN FIRM
Marion Graphics

CLIENT
Organic Theatre Company
DESIGN FIRM
dawn design
DESIGNER
Dawn Peccatiello

CLIENT
Alexandria 5K Race
DESIGN FIRM
Bremmer & Goris Communications
DESIGNERS
Li-Chou, Miki Lo

CLIENT
d3cg
DESIGN FIRM
re: salzman designs
DESIGNERS
Ida Cheinman, Rick Salzman

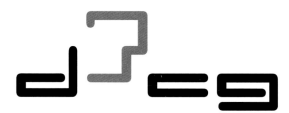

CLIENT
MS Ballin Investments
DESIGN FIRM
Guarino Graphics & Design Studio
DESIGNER
Jan Guarino

CLIENT
Sony
DESIGN FIRM
Phoenix Design Works
DESIGNERS
James M. Skiles, Rod Ollerenshaw

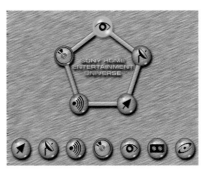

CLIENT
Phil Anders Clinical Message Therapist
DESIGN FIRM
Ray Dugas Design
DESIGNER
Ray B. Dugas

CLIENT
Government of British Columbia
DESIGN FIRM
Holly Dickens Design
DESIGNER
Holly Dickens

CLIENT
dialogue3
DESIGN FIRM
dialogue3
DESIGNER
John V. Clarke

CLIENT
Arkansas Razorbacks
DESIGN FIRM
Phoenix Design Works
DESIGNER
James M. Skiles

CLIENT
Operations & Plant Managers Association
DESIGN FIRM
Minx Design
DESIGNER
Cecilia M. Sveda

CLIENT
Urban Ecology Institute
DESIGN FIRM
CA Design
DESIGNERS
Cheryl Allen, Tony Persiani

CLIENT
Center for Tobacco Cessation
DESIGN FIRM
Graves Fowler Associates
DESIGNER
Viviane Moritz

CLIENT
Children's Museum of Pittsburgh
DESIGN FIRM
Brady Communications
DESIGNERS
Jim Bolander, Bill Bittner,
Bryan Brunsell

CLIENT
Western Growers Association
DESIGN FIRM
Lawrence & Ponder Ideaworks
DESIGNERS
Marvie Blair, Jim Bell, Bil Dicks,
Gary Frederickson, Lynda Lawrence

CLIENT
Altrio
DESIGN FIRM
Hamagami/Carroll
DESIGNER
Paul Wasilewski

CLIENT
Dept. of Parks & Recreation,
Jeffersonville, IN.
DESIGN FIRM
Smith Design Associates
DESIGNER
Cheryl Smith

CLIENT
Kellogg Foundation
DESIGN FIRM
Levine & Associates
DESIGNER
Lena Markley

CLIENT
Enviroll
DESIGN FIRM
Jodi Britt Designs
DESIGNER
Jodi Britt

CLIENT
National Starch and Chemical Company
DESIGN FIRM
Alchemy Consulting & Design
DESIGNER
Tracy Hubbard

CLIENT
Wes Morton
DESIGN FIRM
Liska + Associates, Inc.
DESIGNER
Steve Liska

CLIENT
Sun Orchard Brand
DESIGN FIRM
McElveney & Palozzi Design Group
DESIGNER
Jon Westfall

CLIENT
The McKnight Group
DESIGN FIRM
Kolano Design
DESIGNER
Cate Sides

McKnight

CLIENT
Ojo Photography
DESIGNER
Jenny Kolcun

Ojo Photography

CLIENT
The Coast Connection
DESIGN FIRM
Hubbell Design Works
DESIGNER
Leighton Hubbell

CLIENT
Ubisoft
DESIGN FIRM
Peñabrand/Butler, Shine + Stern
DESIGNER
Luis Peña

Tom Clancy's

CLIENT
Esteam
DESIGN FIRM
Desbrow
DESIGNERS
Kimberly Miller,
Brian Lee Campbell

CLIENT
Robinson Knife Company
DESIGN FIRM
Michael Orr + Associates
DESIGNERS
Michael R. Orr,
Thomas Freeland

the original
Chip Clip®

CLIENT
Integrated Construction Services
DESIGN FIRM
Marcia Herrmann Design
DESIGNER
Marcia Herrmann

CLIENT
Rice n Roll
DESIGN FIRM
Monster Design
DESIGNER
Theresa Veranth

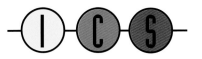

Integrated Construction Services

ricenroll SOUP SUSHI SALAD

CLIENT
Pacific Institute of
Community Organizations
DESIGN FIRM
Graves Fowler Associates
DESIGNER
Victoria Q. Robinson

CLIENT
Rocamojo
DESIGN FIRM
Evenson Design Group
DESIGNER
Stan Evenson

PICO California

CLIENT
Idyllwilde
DESIGN FIRM
Greenhaus
DESIGNERS
Tracy Sabin,
Craig Fuller,
Sandra Sharp

DESIGN FIRM
Portfolio Center
DESIGNER
Bruce MacLean

Idyllwilde
PARKER COLORADO

BEIJING
2008

CLIENT
Drs. Marc Cohen & Nancy Swartz
DESIGN FIRM
Randi Wolf Design
DESIGNER
Randi Wolf

Marc S. Cohen, MD, FACS • Nancy G. Swartz, MS, MD, FACS
Ophthalmic Plastic and Cosmetic Surgeons

CLIENT
Appleseed Beads Co.
DESIGN FIRM
Lemley Design Company
DESIGNERS
David Lemley,
Yuri Shvets,
Matthew Loyd

CLIENT
Alliance
DESIGN FIRM
Never Boring Design
DESIGNERS
Cheryl Cernigoj,
David Boring

CLIENT
Animal Adventure
DESIGN FIRM
Capsule
DESIGNER
Dan Baggenstoss

CLIENT
Resource Graphic
DESIGN FIRM
Pressley Jacobs
DESIGNER
Sarah Lin

CLIENT
Fred Munnell Designs
DESIGN FIRM
Ave Design Studio
DESIGNER
Mary Ann Cole

CLIENT
FreeMotion
DESIGN FIRM
Hornall Anderson Design Works, Inc.
DESIGNERS
Jack Anderson, Kathy Saito,
Sonja Max, Henry Yiu,
Alan Copeland

CLIENT
Crescent Street Coffee
DESIGN FIRM
Portfolio Center
DESIGNER
David Zorne

CLIENT
PatchMail
DESIGN FIRM
Larsen Design + Interactive
DESIGNERS
Paul Wharton, Todd Nesser,
Jon Thomas

CLIENT
Emaar Properties
DESIGN FIRM
Futurebrand Hypermedia
DESIGNER
Nicole Sokoloff

CLIENT
Wight
DESIGN FIRM
Steele
DESIGNERS
Scott Steele,
Paula Zimmer

CLIENT
Gunn Automotive
DESIGN FIRM
Toolbox Studios, Inc.
DESIGNERS
Stan McElrath,
Paul Soupiset,
Eddie Tamez

CLIENT
Dunkin' Donuts
DESIGN FIRM
Hill Holliday Advertising
DESIGNER
Mina Kalemkeryan

CLIENT
Morrow Engineering, Inc.
DESIGN FIRM
Craghead + Harrold
DESIGNER
Shawn Stuckey

strawberry
COOLATTA™

MORROW ENGINEERING, INC.

CLIENT
Midwest Power System
DESIGN FIRM
X Design Company
DESIGNER
Alex Valderrama

CLIENT
Formtek
DESIGN FIRM
Sightline Marketing
DESIGNERS
Samantha Guerry,
Clay Marshall

CLIENT
The Chaffee Zoo
DESIGN FIRM
Shields Design
DESIGNER
Charles Shields,
Scott Severance

CLIENT
Hunt Associates
DESIGN FIRM
Shea, Inc.
DESIGNER
Holly Robbins

CLIENT
Rubin Postaer Direct
DESIGN FIRM
Evenson Design Group
DESIGNERS
Mark Sojka, John Han,
Stan Evenson

CLIENT
New England Foundation for the Arts
DESIGN FIRM
RainCastle Communications
DESIGNER
Rotem Meller

New England
Foundation
for the Arts

CLIENT
Xtreme Center
DESIGN FIRM
Dula Image Group
DESIGNER
Michael Dula

CLIENT
Information Technology Training Inst.
DESIGN FIRM
Ave Design Studio
DESIGNER
Adriana Romero

CLIENT
Dog Dish—Bill Handy
DESIGN FIRM
Walsh Associates, Inc.
DESIGNER
Jared Milan

CLIENT
Coronado Builders
DESIGN FIRM
GCG
DESIGNER
Iva Gur

CLIENT
CYKO Inc.
DESIGN FIRM
X Design Company
DESIGNERS
Alex Valderrama,
Doug Applegate

CLIENT
SBC Communications Inc.
DESIGN FIRM
Rodgers Townsend
DESIGNER
Kris Wright

CLIENT
Kurt West Design
DESIGN FIRM
Buttitta Design
DESIGNER
Patti Buttitta

CLIENT
Green Bay Packers
DESIGN FIRM
ZD Studios, Inc.
DESIGNERS
Mark Schmitz,
Tina Remy

CLIENT
Atomic Vegetarian
DESIGN FIRM
Portfolio Center
DESIGNER
Christian Helms

CLIENT
NYSRS—New York State Restaurant Services
DESIGN FIRM
Pisarkiewicz Mazor & Co., Inc.
DESIGNERS
Dan Bartels, Candice Waddell,
Mary Pisarkiewicz

Smoke-Free Homes

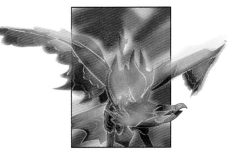

CLIENT
Clare Bridge
DESIGN FIRM
Bridge Creative
DESIGNER
Alexander Bridge

CLIENT
Palace Casino Resort
DESIGN FIRM
The Prime Time Group
DESIGNERS
John Seymour,
Ted Riemann

CLIENT
Sunaroma
DESIGN FIRM
Mainframe Media & Design LLC
DESIGNER
Lucinda Wei

CLIENT
Cigarhombre
DESIGN FIRM
Smith Design Associates
DESIGNER
Cheryl Smith

SUNAROMA

cigarhombre

CLIENT
Girl Scouts of America
DESIGN FIRM
Thompson Design Group
DESIGNERS
Dennis Thompson,
Elizabeth Berta

CLIENT
Evangel Cathedral
DESIGN FIRM
Addison Whitney
DESIGNER
Trey Walsh,
Kimberlee Davis,
Kelly Brewster

ONE WARM COAT

CLIENT
Georgetown University Alumni Assoc.
DESIGN FIRM
Lomangino Studio Inc.
DESIGNER
Kristina Bonner

CLIENT
Southwest Restaurant Management Inc.
DESIGN FIRM
Ellen Bruss Design
DESIGNERS
Ellen Bruss,
Charles Carpenter,
Greg Carr

CLIENT
Congruence/Jan Torrisi-Mokwa
DESIGN FIRM
Berkeley Design LLC
DESIGNER
Larry Torno

CONGRUENCE

CLIENT
Connectables
DESIGN FIRM
Avenue Group
DESIGNERS
Mike Gorgo,
Geoffrey Mark,
Bob Domenz

connectables

CLIENT
Sunbless Harvest International Co., Ltd.
DESIGN FIRM
Y & P Design
International Inc.
DESIGNER
Wenping Hsiao

CLIENT
Mohona Restaurant
DESIGN FIRM
Portfolio Center
DESIGNER
David Zorne

CLIENT
Riverdeep
DESIGN FIRM
Gill Fishman Associates
DESIGNER
Alicia Ozyjowski,
Gill Fishman

CLIENT
Eugene Parks & Open Spaces
DESIGN FIRM
Funk/Levis
& Associates
DESIGNERS
Beverly Soasey,
David Funk

CLIENT
Wendy Gage
DESIGN FIRM
Gage Design
DESIGNER
Chris Roberts

CLIENT
Dawson Communications
DESIGN FIRM
Susan Northrop Design
DESIGNER
Susan Northrop

CLIENT
32 Good Reasons, Family Dentistry
DESIGN FIRM
Perlman Company
DESIGNER
Robert Perlman

CLIENT
Gannon Electric
DESIGN FIRM
ZGraphics, Ltd.
DESIGNER
Nate Baron,
Joe Zeller

CLIENT
Strategic Branding International, LLC
DESIGN FIRM
Adam Filippo + Associates
DESIGNERS
Blair Good,
Ralph James Russini

CLIENT
Cygnet Risk Management
DESIGN FIRM
Leigh Maida Graphic Design
DESIGNER
Leigh Maida

STRATEGIC BRANDING INTERNATIONAL, LLC.

CLIENT
Toledo Public Schools
DESIGN FIRM
Lesniewicz Associates
DESIGNERS
Les Adams, Terrence Lesniewicz

CLIENT
Dog Paw Pet Supply Store
DESIGN FIRM
Ries Creativity

CLIENT
Green Bay Packers
DESIGN FIRM
ZD Studios, Inc.
DESIGNERS
Mark Schmitz,
Tina Remy

CLIENT
OneSphere
DESIGN FIRM
Miller Brooks, Inc.
DESIGNERS
Dan Henne,
Joanne Johnson

CLIENT
TCU Ballet & Modern Dance
DESIGN FIRM
Atomic Design
DESIGNER
Lewis Glaser

CLIENT
AIGA Las Vegas Chapter
DESIGN FIRM
M3ad.com
DESIGNER
Dan McElhattan III

CLIENT
Yo Yo Micro
DESIGN FIRM
McGee Design
DESIGNER
Kelly McGee

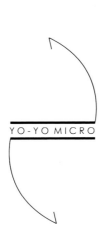

CLIENT
Kanaka Peak
DESIGN FIRM
Full Steam Marketing
DESIGNER
Lori Hughes

CLIENT
Putting Courses of America
DESIGN FIRM
Dula Image Group
DESIGNER
Michael Dula

CLIENT
National Mining Association
DESIGN FIRM
HC Creative Communications
DESIGNER
Jessica Vogel

BISHOP'S EDUCATION FUND
Heart, Mind & Spirit
for the

jm web design

Fish Market

GREAT WISCONSIN
ROAD TRIP

BROKAW
Rising by the River

GENERESSENCE®
indulgent collection

BANGKOK

EMIRATES LIVING

MICHAEL K. DE NEVE & Co
CONSTRUCTION CONSULTANTS

SOJOURNA
PRODUCTIONS
Stories Worth Telling

ReVolution™

ACBS

Information. Insight. Solutions.

POWERVIEW

dwelling

the home idea place

INSITE WORKS   ARCHITECTURE
SITE DESIGN DEVELOPMENT

WRIGHT
AT HOME
LLC

CLIENT
Howell & Vancuren
DESIGN FIRM
Walsh Associates, Inc.
DESIGNER
Jared Milam

CLIENT
Beithan, Hessler Corporate Communications
DESIGN FIRM
Eiche, Oehjne Design Gbr
DESIGNERS
Tracy Sabin,
Peter Oehjne

CLIENT
Second Nature
DESIGN FIRM
Never Boring Design
DESIGNER
Sarah Oro

CLIENT
Biotechnology
Industry Organization
DESIGN FIRM
Kircher, Inc.
DESIGNER
Bruce E. Morgan

CLIENT
Technology Secure Corporation
DESIGN FIRM
Deka Design
DESIGNERS
Dmitry Krasny

CLIENT
Crayola/Binney & Smith
DESIGN FIRM
Evenson Design Group
DESIGNERS
Kera Scott,
Glenn Sakamoto
Stan Evenson

CLIENT
Wirestone
DESIGN FIRM
Dula Image Group
DESIGNER
Michael Dula

CLIENT
Apian Software
DESIGN FIRM
Platform Creative Group
DESIGNER
Jin Kwon

CLIENT
Lund Food Holdings
DESIGN FIRM
Capsule
DESIGNERS
Dan Baggenstoss,
Greg Brose,
Brian Adducci

BYERLY'S.

CLIENT
Mega Holdings
DESIGN FIRM
Y & P Design

CLIENT
Warner Books/6th Avenue Books
DESIGNER
Jackie Merri Meyer

CLIENT
TH!NK—The Business of Meetings:
Alliance Service Network
DESIGN FIRM
Kircher, Inc.
DESIGNER
Bruce E. Morgan

CLIENT
Blatstein Consulting Group
DESIGN FIRM
Art 270, Inc.
DESIGNER
Nicole Ganz

CLIENT
Nutrition 21
DESIGN FIRM
Planit
DESIGNERS
Jon Klemstine, Molly Stevenson

(chromium picolinate)

CLIENT
San Diego Eye Center
DESIGN FIRM
Hetz Advertising
DESIGNER
Michael Hetz

SAN
DIEGO
EYE
CENTER

CLIENT
Bottleneck Blues Club
DESIGN FIRM
Visual Asylum
DESIGNERS
Joel Sotelo,
Tracy Sabin

The Concert for New York City

CLIENT
Just J.A.C. Productions
DESIGN FIRM
Keyword Design
DESIGNER
Judith Mayer

CLIENT
Palace Casino Resort
DESIGN FIRM
The Prime Time Group
DESIGNER
Hugh Ricks

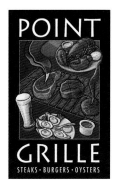

CLIENT
Tortue
DESIGN FIRM
Premier Communications
Group
DESIGNERS
Randy Fossano,
Kate Pultz

CLIENT
Act2L
DESIGN FIRM
Keen Branding
DESIGNER
Mike Raveney

CLIENT
CT Horizons, LLC
DESIGN FIRM
Indicia Design, Inc.
DESIGNER
Ryan Hembree

CLIENT
Mitchell Group
DESIGN FIRM
Archer Communications, Inc.
DESIGNER
Frank Argento

CLIENT
Saint Andrews School
DESIGN FIRM
GCG Advertising
DESIGNER
Brian Wilburn

CLIENT
The Institute for
Responsible Citizenship
DESIGN FIRM
Schum & Associates
DESIGNERS
Ephraim Schum,
Guy Schum

CLIENT
Dunkin' Donuts
DESIGN FIRM
Hill Holliday
DESIGNER
Mina Kalemkeryan

CLIENT
Whitfield Paralegal Services
DESIGN FIRM
Boelts/Stratford Associates
DESIGNERS
Travis Owens,
Jackson Boelts

CLIENT
Timbuk2
DESIGN FIRM
Portfolio Center
DESIGNER
Marshall Wolfe

CLIENT
Juelerie
DESIGN FIRM
Hetz Advertising
DESIGNERS
Michael Hetz,
Pamela Pogue

CLIENT
Barbagelata Construction
DESIGN FIRM
Bondepus Graphic Design
DESIGNER
Gary Epis

CLIENT
Funk Software
DESIGN FIRM
Gill Fishman Associates
DESIGNERS
Michael Persons,
Alicia Ozyjowski,
Gill Fishman

CLIENT
KAZI Beverage Company
DESIGN FIRM
Hornall Anderson Design Works, Inc.
DESIGNERS
Jack Anderson, Larry Anderson, Jay Hilburn,
Kaye Farmer, Henry Yiu,
Mary Chin Hutchison,
Sonja Max,
Dorothee Soechting

CLIENT
Donahue Schriber
DESIGN FIRM
ID8 Studio/RTKL
DESIGNER
Anthony Hsu

CLIENT
Solin Design Architects
DESIGN FIRM
Scott F. Reid + Associates
DESIGNERS
Scott Reid,
Don French

CLIENT
Torrid Clothing
DESIGN FIRM
Portfolio Center
DESIGNER
Gorete Ferreira

T O R R I D

CLIENT
Integrix
DESIGN FIRM
Out Of The Box
DESIGNER
Rick Schneider

CLIENT
Coastal Plastic Surgery
DESIGN FIRM
Parker/White
DESIGNERS
Tracy Sabin,
Cindy White

CLIENT
Impact Referral Group
DESIGN FIRM
Lesniewicz Associates
DESIGNERS
Amy Lesniewicz, Eric Crockett

CLIENT
Turn Key Office Solutions
DESIGN FIRM
Dever Designs
DESIGNER
Jeffrey L. Dever

CLIENT
Intercapital Partners
DESIGN FIRM
Doerr Associates
DESIGNER
Brad Paulson

CLIENT
Green Bay Packers
DESIGN FIRM
ZD Studios, Inc.
DESIGNERS
Mark Schmitz,
Tina Remy

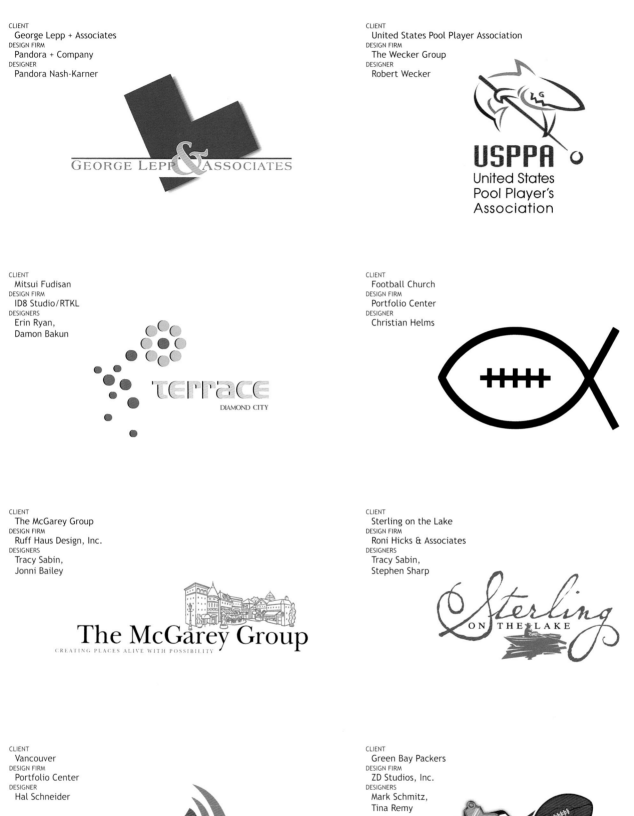

CLIENT
George Lepp + Associates
DESIGN FIRM
Pandora + Company
DESIGNER
Pandora Nash-Karner

CLIENT
United States Pool Player Association
DESIGN FIRM
The Wecker Group
DESIGNER
Robert Wecker

CLIENT
Mitsui Fudisan
DESIGN FIRM
ID8 Studio/RTKL
DESIGNERS
Erin Ryan,
Damon Bakun

CLIENT
Football Church
DESIGN FIRM
Portfolio Center
DESIGNER
Christian Helms

CLIENT
The McGarey Group
DESIGN FIRM
Ruff Haus Design, Inc.
DESIGNERS
Tracy Sabin,
Jonni Bailey

CLIENT
Sterling on the Lake
DESIGN FIRM
Roni Hicks & Associates
DESIGNERS
Tracy Sabin,
Stephen Sharp

CLIENT
Vancouver
DESIGN FIRM
Portfolio Center
DESIGNER
Hal Schneider

CLIENT
Green Bay Packers
DESIGN FIRM
ZD Studios, Inc.
DESIGNERS
Mark Schmitz,
Tina Remy

CLIENT
South African Airways
DESIGNERS
Claude Salzberger,
Carlos Sanchez

CLIENT
Henri Matisse
DESIGN FIRM
Portfolio Center
DESIGNER
Debbie Disney

CLIENT
Andra Patzholdt
DESIGN FIRM
Design Guys
DESIGNERS
Steven Sikora,
Anne Peterson

CLIENT
Melissa Stevens Image Consultant
DESIGN FIRM
Indicia Design, Inc.
DESIGNER
Ryan Hembree

CLIENT
RBC
DESIGNERS
Michael Thibodeaw,
Tony Enns

CLIENT
B'nai B'rith Youth Organization
DESIGN FIRM
Beth Singer Design
DESIGNERS
Suheun Yu,
Chris Hoth

CLIENT
Green Bay Packers
DESIGN FIRM
ZD Studios, Inc.
DESIGNERS
Mark Schmitz,
Tina Remy

CLIENT
Classic Thrift
DESIGN FIRM
Portfolio Center
DESIGNER
Christian Helms

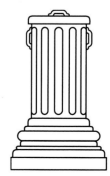

CLIENT
Paul Hartmann
DESIGN FIRM
Rabil + Bates Design Co.
DESIGNER
Seth Sirbaugh

CLIENT
the Juniper Martini Bar
DESIGN FIRM
Asylum
DESIGNER
Erin Wright

CLIENT
VIA Bowling Products
DESIGN FIRM
Funk/Levis & Associates
DESIGNER
Alex Wijnen

CLIENT
Iteration Z
DESIGN FIRM
Dula Image Group
DESIGNER
Michael Dula

CLIENT
St. Mary's County Government
DESIGN FIRM
Rottman Creative Group, LLC
DESIGNERS
Gary Rottman,
Jenna Holcombe

CLIENT
Rubin Cordaro Design
DESIGN FIRM
Rubin Cordaro Design
DESIGNER
Jim Cordaro

CLIENT
Cypress Financial Consultants, LLC
DESIGN FIRM
Archer Communications, Inc.
DESIGNER
Frank Argento

CLIENT
Extasis
DESIGN FIRM
Portfolio Center
DESIGNER
Anna Lazaws

CLIENT
Rt 66
DESIGN FIRM
Portfolio Center
DESIGNER
Christian Helms

CLIENT
IFF International Flavors & Fragrances
DESIGN FIRM
AJF Marketing
DESIGNER
Justin Brindisi

CAPLOCK

CLIENT
United Glass &
Panel Systems, Inc.
DESIGN FIRM
Innis Maggiore Group
DESIGNER
Jeff Monter

United Glass
& Panel Systems, Inc.

CLIENT
Golden Retriever Rescue of Michigan
DESIGN FIRM
Lesniewicz Associates
DESIGNER
Amy Lesniewicz

CLIENT
Hyatt Regency Huntington Beach
DESIGN FIRM
David Carter Design Assoc.
DESIGNER
Rachel Graham

RED CHAIR LOUNGE

CLIENT
University of North Carolina
DESIGN FIRM
Lipman-Hearne
DESIGNERS
Tracy Sabin, Victoria Primicias

UNIVERSITY
OF NORTH
CAROLINA
CHAPEL HILL

CLIENT
Keen Branding
DESIGN FIRM
Keen Branding
DESIGNERS
Mike Raveney,
Alicia Stack

keen branding

CLIENT
SimpleGov.com
DESIGN FIRM
Hetz Advertising
DESIGNER
Michael Hetz

SIMPLEGOV.COM

Because online is better than in line.

Gambrinus Co./Shiner Bock
DESIGN FIRM
Toolbox Studios, Inc.
DESIGNERS
Paul Soupiset,
Stan McElrath

CLIENT
Hyatt Regency Huntington Beach
DESIGN FIRM
David Carter Design Assoc.
DESIGNER
Stephanie Burt

CLIENT
Republic Engineered Products
DESIGN FIRM
Innis Maggiore Group
DESIGNER
Jef Monter

CLIENT
Crisp & Associates
DESIGN FIRM
Never Boring Design
DESIGNER
Sarah Oro

CLIENT
El Rio Foundation
DESIGN FIRM
Boelts/Stratford Associates
DESIGNERS
Jackson Boelts,
Kerry Stratford

CLIENT
Synaptics
DESIGN FIRM
Portfolio Center
DESIGNER
Christian Helms

CLIENT
Springfield Youth Farm
DESIGN FIRM
Defteling Design
DESIGNER
Alex Wijnen

CLIENT
Crew Construction Corp.
DESIGN FIRM
Acme Communications, Inc.
DESIGNER
Kiki Boucher

CLIENT
Houston, Tx
DESIGN FIRM
Portfolio Center
DESIGNER
Marshall Wolfe

CLIENT
Women's Care Physicians & Surgeons
DESIGN FIRM
Funk/Levis & Associates
DESIGNERS
Beverly Soasey,
Joan Madden,
Lada Korol

CLIENT
Dayberries Bakery & Cafe
DESIGN FIRM
Hornall Anderson Design Works, Inc.
DESIGNERS
Mary Hermes, Mary Chin Hutchison,
Hillary Radbill

CLIENT
Powerline
DESIGN FIRM
Portfolio Center
DESIGNER
Marshall Wolfe

CLIENT
Greenlight Construction
DESIGN FIRM
Portfolio Center
DESIGNER
Christian Helms

CLIENT
Texas Jack Jean Co.
DESIGN FIRM
Out Of The Box
DESIGNER
Rick Schneider

CLIENT
Idyllwild Area Historical Society
DESIGN FIRM
Evenson Design Group
DESIGNERS
Mark Sojka,
Stan Evenson

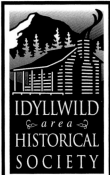

CLIENT
Mitem Corporation
DESIGN FIRM
Clark Creative Group
DESIGNERS
Annemarie Clark,
Thurlow Washam

CLIENT
Smart Card Corporate
DESIGN FIRM
Y & P Design
DESIGNER
Wenping Hsiao

CLIENT
Mike Dupuy Falconry
DESIGN FIRM
Bruce E. Morgan Graphic Design
DESIGNER
Bruce E. Morgan

CLIENT
City of Arcadia
DESIGN FIRM
ID8 Studio/RTKL
DESIGNER
Anthony Hsu

CLIENT
Forever Young
DESIGN FIRM
Never Boring Design
DESIGNER
Sarah Oro

CLIENT
The Copper Beech Inn
DESIGN FIRM
Primary Design, Inc.
DESIGNERS
Allison Davis,
Jules Epstein

CLIENT
Tell Me a Story...
DESIGN FIRM
Defteling Design
DESIGNER
Alex Wijnen

CLIENT
Topaz Partners
DESIGN FIRM
Gill Fishman Associates
DESIGNERS
Tammy Torrey,
Gill Fishman

CLIENT
820 Technologies
DESIGN FIRM
GCG Advertising
DESIGNER
Bill Buck

CLIENT
Soulo
DESIGN FIRM
Portfolio Center
DESIGNER
Amanda MacCauley

CLIENT
Freerein
DESIGN FIRM
Hornall Anderson Design Works, Inc.
DESIGNERS
Jack Anderson, Mark Popich, John Anicker,
Tobi Brown, Steffanie Lorig, Bruce Stigler,
Ensi Mofasser, Elmer dela Cruz, John Anderle,
Gretchen Cook

CLIENT
Southside Nazarene Church
DESIGN FIRM
Mickey Moore + Associates
DESIGNER
Mickey Moore

CLIENT
Irvine Company
DESIGN FIRM
ID8 Studio/RTKL
DESIGNER
Kevin Horn

CLIENT
Sciovox, Inc.
DESIGN FIRM
Portfolio Center
DESIGNER
Amanda MacCauley

CLIENT
Racing for Recovery
DESIGN FIRM
Lesniewicz Associates
DESIGNER
Amy Lesniewicz

CLIENT
Goodnight Moon
DESIGN FIRM
Capsule
DESIGNER
Anchalee Chambundabongse

CLIENT
Youngstown Metropolitan
Housing Authority
DESIGN FIRM
Innis Maggiore Group
DESIGNER
Jeff Monter

CLIENT
Round House Theatre
DESIGN FIRM
Kircher, Inc.
DESIGNER
Bruce E. Morgan

CLIENT
Deepwell
DESIGN FIRM
designRoom Creative
DESIGNER
Chad Gordon

CLIENT
Pittsburgh Downtown Partnership
DESIGN FIRM
Elias/Savion Advertising
DESIGNER
Rachel Arnold

PITTSBURGH

DOWNTOWN

PARTNERSHIP

CLIENT
Palace Entertainment
DESIGN FIRM
ID8 Studio/RTKL
DESIGNER
Amy Owen

CLIENT
Anne Arunde/County Dept. of Health
DESIGN FIRM
Crosby Marketing Communications
DESIGNER
Carol Barry

Campaign for Healthier Restaurants

CLIENT
KreativWerks
DESIGN FIRM
McMillian Design
DESIGNER
William McMillian

CLIENT
NA Kitee Properties
DESIGN FIRM
Futurebrand Hypermedia
DESIGNER
Christiano Andriotti

Jumeirah Islands

CLIENT
Beijing 2008
DESIGN FIRM
Portfolio Center
DESIGNER
Louis Bravo

BEIJING
2008

CLIENT
ira Wexler
DESIGN FIRM
Rabil + Bates Design Co.
DESIGNER
Seth Sirbaugh

CLIENT
Michael Rubin Architects
DESIGN FIRM
Acme Communications, Inc.
DESIGNER
Kiki Boucher

MICHAEL RUBIN
ARCHITECTS

CLIENT
Soneva Fushi
DESIGN FIRM
Portfolio Center
DESIGNER
Hal Schnieder

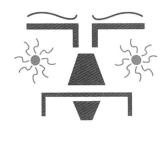

SONEVA FUSHI

CLIENT
Western Illinois University
DESIGN FIRM
Lipman Hearne
DESIGNERS
Tracy Sabin,
Victoria Primicias

CLIENT
Pembroke Real Estate
DESIGN FIRM
Doerr Associates
DESIGNER
Brad Paulson

OAK GROVE
V I L L A G E

CLIENT
Pislets Clothing
DESIGN FIRM
Portfolio Center
DESIGNER
Piper Moore

CLIENT
Keller/CMS, Inc. RiverPark Development
DESIGN FIRM
ID8 Studio/RTKL
DESIGNERS
Amy Owen,
Steve Kelly

RIVERPARK

CLIENT
Benjamin Rose
DESIGN FIRM
Karen Skunta & Company
DESIGNERS
Karen Skunta,
Christopher Suster,
Ron Kurtz

CLIENT
Lane County Waste Management
DESIGN FIRM
Funk/Levis & Associates
DESIGNERS
Christopher Berner,
Lada Korol

less *is best*

CLIENT
Homeless Children's Education Fund
DESIGN FIRM
Elias/Savion Advertising
DESIGNER
Rachel Arnold

HOMELESS
CHILDREN'S
EDUCATION
FUND

CLIENT
  MPS Group
DESIGN FIRM
  Addison Whitney
DESIGNERS
  Kimberlee Davis,
  Lisa Johnston,
  David Houk

CLIENT
  Attenex Corporation
DESIGN FIRM
  Hornall Anderson Design Works, Inc.
DESIGNERS
  Katha Dalton,
  Jana Wilson Esser

CLIENT
  Jump Start Communications, Inc.
DESIGN FIRM
  Gage Design
DESIGNER
  Chris Roberts

CLIENT
  C-Cap (Careers Through
  Culinary Arts Program)
DESIGN FIRM
  Deka Design
DESIGNERS
  Dmitry Krasny,
  Tali Krakowsky

CLIENT
  MedPlans Partners, Inc.
DESIGN FIRM
  Indicia Design, Inc.
DESIGNERS
  Ryan Hembree,
  Clark Bystrom

CLIENT
  WD40
DESIGN FIRM
  Portfolio Center
DESIGNER
  Brandi Clark

CLIENT
Verge Wireless Systems, Inc.
DESIGN FIRM
Gage Design
DESIGNER
Chris Roberts

CLIENT
Stratus Masonry Company, Inc.
DESIGN FIRM
Planit
DESIGNER
Jan Klemstine

STRATUS

MASONRY COMPANY, INC.

CLIENT
Duket, Porter, MacPherson
DESIGN FIRM
Lesniewicz Associates
DESIGNERS
Les Adams,
Terrence Lesniewicz

CLIENT
Rockdale Hospital Logo
DESIGN FIRM
Jones Worley Design, Inc.
DESIGNER
Michael Sater

DUKET|PORTER|MacPHERSON

ROCKDALE
HOSPITAL
& HEALTH SYSTEM

CLIENT
Hammer Golf Performance & Fitness
DESIGN FIRM
The Wecker Group
DESIGNER
Robert Wecker

CLIENT
Fleet Bank
DESIGNER
Greg Silveria

HAMMER GOLF
PERFORMANCE & FITNESS

CLIENT
Lake Erie Alpacas
DESIGN FIRM
Lesniewicz Associates
DESIGNER
Amy Lesniewicz

CLIENT
El Conquistador Resort & Country Club
DESIGN FIRM
Parkhurst Design
DESIGNER
Denis Parkhurst

CLIENT
SPG3
DESIGN FIRM
Art 270, Inc.
DESIGNERS
Sagan Medvec,
Carl Mill

DESIGN FIRM
Primary Design, Inc.
DESIGNERS
Jules Epstein,
Jasmine Gillingham

CLIENT
O'Dell Engineering
DESIGN FIRM
Never Boring Design
DESIGNER
Cheryl Cernigoj

CLIENT
Caffé Botanica
DESIGN FIRM
Funk/Levis & Associates
DESIGNER
Alex Wijnen

CLIENT
Mill Valley Film Festival
DESIGN FIRM
Futurebrand
DESIGNER
Paul Gardner

CLIENT
Downtowner Woodfire Grille
DESIGN FIRM
Capsule
DESIGNER
Brian Adducci

Mill Valley Film Festival

DOWNTOWNER
-WOODFIRE GRILLE-

CLIENT
Red Wing Shoe Company
DESIGN FIRM
Capsule
DESIGNER
Dan Baggenstoss

CLIENT
Marshall Strategy, Inc.
DESIGN FIRM
Meta Design
DESIGNERS
Brett Wickens,
Neil Sadler

Marshall

CLIENT
Interact Theatre Company
DESIGN FIRM
Art270, Inc.
DESIGNER
Nicole Ganz

CLIENT
MU
DESIGN FIRM
Out Of The Box
DESIGNER
Rick Schneider

INDEX